Moose
on the
Table

Also by Jim Clemmer

THE LEADER'S DIGEST
  Timeless Principles for Team
  and Organization Success

GROWING THE DISTANCE
  Timeless Principles for Personal,
  Career, and Family Success

PATHWAYS TO PERFORMANCE
  A Guide to Transforming Yourself,
  Your Team, and Your Organization

FIRING ON ALL CYLINDERS
  The Service/Quality System for
  High-Powered Corporate Performance

THE VIP STRATEGY
  Leadership Skills for
  Exceptional Performance

Moose
on the
Table

A Novel Approach to
Communications @ Work

Jim Clemmer

**BASTIAN
BOOKS**

Published in 2008 by
Bastian Books
Toronto, Canada
www.bastianbooks.com
A division of Bastian Publishing Services Ltd.

ISBN 978-0-9782221-7-8

Cataloguing in Publication Data available from Library and Archives Canada.

Design and layout: www.WeMakeBooks.ca

Illustrations: William Kimber

Printed in United States of America

Second Printing, 2009

To Heather, Chris, Jenn, and Vanessa
And to our family, friends, and associates

Contents

Preface

No moose were harmed in the writing of this book!
I started using the Moose-on-the-Table metaphor in the mid to late nineties as I helped management teams identify and address the issues that were getting in the way of higher performance. Just like dysfunctional families, many such teams find it easier to avoid tough conversations. But rarely do problems get better when left unaddressed. Rather, the moose grow larger, breed, and increase the size of the herd.

A Moose-on-the-Table section in the Authenticity chapter of my previous book *The Leader's Digest,* along with evolving moose-hunting workshops and executive retreats, accelerated The CLEMMER Group's use of this metaphor and approach with our Clients. I have amassed a collection of moose memorabilia in my office and T-shirts in my closets. Some have come from friends, family, and associates, because I seem to have become known as "the moose guy."

During a summer family vacation in Prince Edward Island, Heather purchased a fridge magnet for me. It couldn't have been more timely or appropriate, since I was just finishing this manuscript. A cartoon on the magnet showed two moose sipping brews (likely Moosehead beer) in a bar. One of the moose is pointing at a moose's head mounted on the wall behind them. The bubble above his head reads, "Hey! Wait a minute! That's *Jim!*" What are the odds?

Most of my moose memorabilia are from Clients. Many have used the moose approach to playfully open up tough conversations and deal with long-standing issues that had been avoided, ignored, or glossed over. But some teams actually made their situation worse by turning everyone's attention to communication issues and then doing little or nothing to dig out and address the root causes of their problems.

Cowardice and Courage

This book explores the fear–courage continuum through the struggles and experiences of the central character, Pete Leonard. We all have fears of some sort, and what a cunning and stealthy force they are in our personal and organizational lives. Fear is the major cause of most of our stress and worry. And it's an inside job. No one else can make us stressed or worried without our agreement. When we allow fear and worry into our thoughts, they cast huge shadows over our lives and block out the light of the daily enjoyments we could be basking in. These shadows can creep over us and reduce our lives to just barely coping or just getting by. Fear kills team and organizational effectiveness as communications close down and conversations become ever more guarded and shallow.

Like a spotlight cutting through darkness, courage shines brightest in the presence of fear. It's easy to boldly march forward when we're filled with confidence and the way forward is fairly smooth. It's takes real courage – and strong leadership – to navigate our way when we're full of negative fantasies and everything seems to be against us. True courage is to master, rather than be mastered by, our fears.

Victory in difficult circumstances starts with our own victory over self. The best way out of a tough situation is working through it. Thucydides, the ancient Greek historian and the author of the *History of the Peloponnesian War* (covering the battle between Sparta and Athens from 431 to 404 B.C.), declares, "But the bravest are surely those who have the clearest vision of what is before them, glory and danger alike, and yet not withstanding go out and meet it."

A Novel Approach

As the subtitle indicates, I've taken a very different approach with this book. This is my first work of fiction. I began loosely assembling ideas, possible storylines, and potential characters a few years before beginning to write. But I struggled with how to pull it all together.

Then I saw a promotion for a writer's workshop featuring Hollywood story consultant Christopher Vogel. He has evaluated over ten thousand screenplays for major motion picture studios and is the author of the extremely helpful book *The Writer's Journey: Mythic Structure for Writers.* Christopher's consulting success and book are based on a simplification and modernization of Joseph Campbell's 1949 classic *The Hero with a Thousand Faces.* I had previously been inspired by Campbell's study of the hero's journey and transformation through virtually all the mythologies of the world across all cultures and throughout time. He identified one archetypal hero in all of them. George Lucas based his *Star Wars* series on Campbell's work. Since I had found those movies to be profoundly spiritual and entertaining – and Lucas did okay with them – I thought there might be something to learn at the workshop.

Featuring Christopher Vogel and led by writing consultant Sam Horn, the workshop clicked all the pieces magically into place for me. And it didn't hurt that the session was at a lush Cancun beach resort in January either! I came back from the writing retreat inspired and began to spin the tale now before you whenever I could squeeze in a few early-morning hours of writing (my most creative time of the day).

I've thoroughly enjoyed studying and applying the timeless art of storytelling to allow you to be a fly-on-the-wall witness to many of the kinds of ineffective and effective conversations and actions I've seen during my twenty-five years in the personal, team, and organizational-development fields. I had lots of fun writing this book and tried to balance a humorous and engaging story with leadership learning. I hope you find it highly "edutaining."

With Gratitude

It's always tough to acknowledge everyone who has contributed to a book like this, but let me mention the main ones. Heather, my wonderful life and business partner, is my best friend, confidante, counselor, and highly valued business co-owner. She's also the nurturing mother of our three terrific offspring (it's hard to call them kids now), Chris, Jenn, and Vanessa. We are truly blessed to have been entrusted with their childhood and to have seen how they have courageously dealt with life's adversities and challenges as they have grown and matured into thoughtful, successful adults. The closeness and love of our immediate and extended family is a continuous source of energy and renewal for both of us.

Scott Schweyer and Karen Lee have been doing an outstanding job of helping CLEMMER Group Clients blaze their own pathways to higher performance as described in the later chapters of this book. Our years of successful progress have been mutually rewarding for everyone involved and have helped shape many of the key effective approaches described here. Mark Henderson and Derek Mendham contributed highly useful experiences to our early consulting and training work.

Betty Kaita, Darlene Mashinter, Gini Kechnie-Williams, Joanne Savoy, and Cara Tavares provide the invaluable administrative backbone that holds our business together. We have built much of this infrastructure, along with our web site and digital communications, on the great pioneering work of Julie Gil.

I am very thankful to Aidan Crawford for his rare combination of technological expertise – used in our web site and digital communications strategies – and writing skills. His creativity in polishing the rough manuscript and now promoting this book has been invaluable. Don Bastian, an excellent thirty-year veteran editor, was very helpful in streamlining the manuscript. He gently pried the stuffy sections, puffy paragraphs, wandering sentences, and what I thought was a killer ending worthy of a major literary prize from my clenched hands.

In nearly three decades of work with hundreds of Clients, I've been privileged to learn so much from thousands of keynote audience members, workshop and retreat participants, web site visitors, and monthly e-newsletter and book readers. The characters and situations found in this book come directly or indirectly from that deep flowing river of experience. Some of the people you'll meet in this book are composite characters cobbled together from this rich and varied "database."

If you want to know what I'm up to today, you can always visit my web site, **www.clemmer.net**. Along with my blog, you'll find dozens of video clips, hundreds of free articles, and information about my other books, workshops, keynotes, and The CLEMMER Group's consulting services. You can also subscribe to my popular monthly newsletter and Improvement Points e-mail tips service (both are no charge).

I'd love to get your feedback on this book. Visit **www.mooseonthetable.com** to send me your comments and to get further background on this book, purchase multiple copies at steep discounts, and explore our related moose-hunting products and services.

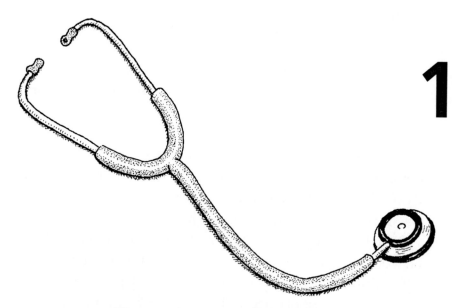

Running on Empty

"Take your shirt off, please," Dr. Yantzi said. "Looks like you've put on a few more pounds. Take deep breaths."

"Whoa, that thing is nice and chilled," Pete said. "Remember, you're the doctor. It's your job to prevent heart attacks, not deliver them by stethoscope."

Dr. Yantzi continued checking Pete's chest. "So what exactly are the symptoms you're experiencing and when did they start?"

"About four o'clock yesterday morning, I woke up with my heart racing, chest pain, and some trouble breathing. I got out of bed, took a stiff drink – for medicinal purposes – and walked around the family room for a while. Things seemed to settle down a bit after that. Michelle came down and wanted me to go to the hospital, but I was feeling a little better and I had far too much to do to spend all morning sitting in a crowded emergency room."

"How are things at work?"

"Oh, the usual. Same crap, different pile. Our company is sliding into the swamp, and my boss isn't doing anything about it."

"And home?"

"Michelle's job is fine – but we hardly see each other these days. Amanda is her usual screaming hormonal self, and Ryan is off at college drinking his way to the bottom of his class. Other than that, things are just peachy."

Pete looked out the window at the gray sky. A fine cold rain blew against the window, leaving beads of water that occasionally gathered and raced down the pane. There weren't any clouds, just a mass of dirty drabness hovering overhead. In the dying afternoon light, the leafless branches of the small tree below were like gray tentacles grasping for the sky.

"What made you decide to come see me today?"

"Last night I hardly slept at all. I was shaky and dizzy and had trouble breathing. I kept having this nightmare of some big animal bearing down on me and crushing my chest against a tree with its big horns. Michelle finally threatened to do even worse if I didn't go the hospital or see you today."

"You can put your shirt back on," Dr. Yantzi said. He sat down at his desk, opened a file, and made a few notes. He motioned Pete to sit across from him.

"I have the lab results from your annual check-up last month," he said. "You're not exactly ready for the Olympics. Your bad cholesterol is very high, you're about fifty pounds overweight, and your blood pressure is way up. It also sounds like you've got a lot of stress in your life at the moment. How much are you drinking these days?"

"I like a glass of wine or beer once in a while."

"How often?"

"Just a couple a day." That couldn't be *too* far off, Pete thought.

"You said you've had a lot of headaches. Are you taking anything for that?"

"I take an occasional pain reliever when it gets real bad." A montage of the large bottles in his bedroom, desk, car, and travel bag flashed before his eyes. He almost reached for a few of the pills he always kept in a plastic case in his coat pocket. Michelle called them his "stress beans" because he ate them like jelly beans.

"I noticed in the paper the other day that NMTS is having financial problems. That must be adding to your stress at work," Dr. Yantzi said in a questioning tone.

Pete thought back to yesterday's conversation with his boss, the senior vice president of client services at Newton-Millbank Tech Services. Pete was the head of that division's operations department. His intrepid leader was not one for making small talk. He led off the conversation with: "We've got a problem in this company right now and we need strong leadership from you to keep your team focused."

Now *that's* rich, Pete thought. He looked at his boss sitting in his overstuffed fake brown leather chair glaring at him through his steel-rimmed glasses – the biggest horse's ass to ever put on a suit and pretend to be a leader, he thought. And now he's going to give me lessons? He stared at the large white letters loudly proclaiming "Doug Drake – Senior Vice President" on the phony gold plaque sitting directly in front of him on Doug's desk.

"I've been reviewing this year's organizational survey results," Doug said, as he picked up a thick report. Little red cellophane flags stuck out of the report like rectangular tongues. They mocked Pete as Doug waved the report up and down. "Trust and communication has really dropped off in your department. No wonder morale is in the basement. Some of the written comments show you've got a very unhappy bunch of campers. That clearly explains why absenteeism is up and our client service levels suck. There's obviously a leadership problem here and I think I'm looking at him."

Then Doug paused for dramatic effect. "What are you going to do about it?"

Pete fidgeted with the Doug Drake desk plaque. "Well, I ... I think there's, uh, a lot of misunderstanding in my department. These survey responses are just their percep-tions; they aren't reality. People just don't understand how much we're doing for them and just how good they have it as the industry goes through this tough time."

"Well, let me give you a dose of reality, Mr. Pete Leonard. If we don't turn this company around, we won't make it through this tough time either. Last month's financials are just in and we're sinking deeper into a big pool of red ink. If we don't reverse this trend now, our creditors will pull the plug or sell us to a competitor. Can you see it, Leonard? The vultures are hovering, and it's up to you to do something before it's feeding time."

Doug grabbed the report and began pacing magisterially around his spacious office. "Your department is the key to holding on to customers," he said. "Your service levels have to improve. I just had a call from Bryon Hammond at Cowersill. I hope you realize they are one of our best cus-tomers. He heard that their technician was leaving us. Bryon thinks his tech walks on water. If he goes, they go with him. With morale levels like the ones in your department, we're not only going to lose some of our best people, we're going to lose our best customers."

Doug gave the giggling red tongues another good shake

for good measure. "You better get control of your department. Show some leadership! Let them know who's boss and just how dire the situation is. Tell them that if they don't start talking to each other and communicate more, we'll all drown together when the ship finally sinks."

Pete ventured in cautiously. "Maybe I should start by reviewing the report and trying to figure out why the scores are so low and what we can do about it."

"For god's sake, man! Do you want the inmates running the asylum? You're the leader. Get in there and shake them up. Make them feel your presence. This isn't the time to go soft. Holding hands and singing Kum Ba Ya just isn't going to cut it. We don't want the workers to see these survey results. That would just add fuel to the fire and make them bitch and moan even more – especially when they see the low communication scores."

Doug landed back in his chair and threw the report on his desk. "If you're not up to the job … Well, let me put it this way: We're looking under every rock and into every cubicle for savings. We're determined to root out each and every expense that isn't adding value to the business. Pete, we're reviewing your job. We need to see you adding value – now!"

"… Earth to Peter. Hello, Peter!"

"Oh, sorry, Doctor. What were you saying?"

"I was asking if the financial problems at NMTS were adding to your stress."

"It's hard to add more water to a glass that's already full and overflowing."

"I see. Well, Peter, I am very concerned about you. If you stay on this road, you're heading for a crash. It might be a heart attack, stroke, or something else. But one thing is clear: it won't be fun for you or your family. The physical factors – like your weight, cholesterol, and blood pressure – are bad enough. But research is now showing that emotional state is a major variable in heart disease and a host of other illnesses. You're not the aggressive and hostile Type A personality that most people think of as high risk."

Pete grabbed onto this statement like a drowning man clutching a piece of driftwood.

"But it looks to me like you're in that equally dangerous category of 'quiet desperation.'"

Pete sank back under the waves.

"I just read about a study of over ten thousand heart-attack victims from dozens of countries. It showed that in the year before their heart attack, most were under much higher levels of stress from work, family, financial, and other factors than a comparable control group. With your severe stress and anxiety, you might as well be a heavy smoker on top of all the other health factors."

"I was once a Type A with some hostility," Pete said. "But it was getting me nowhere and leaving me frustrated. Now I just try to go along to get along."

Dr. Yantzi pulled out his prescription pad. "I am writing you a prescription for antidepressant pills. I hope they can help get you through this tough time in your life. You might want to find a new job, because frankly, Pete, this one is killing you. And you really need to lose some weight and start an exercise program. I'd prescribe pills for that, but Magic Pharmacy is all out."

Pete took the prescription and tried to decipher its squiggles and lines. He folded the paper and put it in his shirt pocket. "Yeah, I guess I do need to get my life in order."

"You sure do. The next time I see you it could be under much more serious circumstances."

Pete poked the elevator button and rocked gently from foot to foot. He took the prescription out of his shirt pocket. Has it come to this? he wondered. Have I reached the point where pharmaceuticals are the only things keeping me going? How did I get here?

He was a few months away from his forty-eighth birthday. His fifteen-year-old daughter, Amanda, and nineteen-year-old son, Ryan, were from his "first big mistake" – his turbulent six-year marriage to Chantal. Chantal and he were both twenty-eight when they got married. They had dated on and off in college and stayed in touch after graduation. She loved his high energy, ambition, athletic skills, and humor. They laughed a lot in that enchanting year before they "tied the noose," as Pete later put it. He loved her beauty, creativity, vigorous independence, and intelligence. They danced, partied, and made love with wild abandon. She could be overbearing at times, but Pete could live with that. When he did push back, Chantal's fiery temper would escalate and sparks would fly. He was always so sorry afterward and would be the first to make up – which would end in passionate fun.

It wasn't clear just when their marriage took a wrong turn, though it may have started before the honeymoon was over. The big fight they had during that Caribbean frolic certainly didn't make for a storybook beginning. Chantal stormed out of their resort room and flew home on her own. Pete followed her and spent the next few days apologizing – although he wasn't quite sure why and for what.

It was the start an all-too-familiar drama played out repetitively over the next six years. Chantal was most irritated when Pete stood his ground and argued with her. That was always certain to end with her exit from his life for a short time. When Ryan was eighteen months old, she took off with him for three days. Pete phoned and drove everywhere he thought she might be. When he finally found her, at her parents' cottage, it took hours of apologizing and pleading to get her to come home. But once Ryan was tucked in and asleep, they had an enthusiastic make-up session in their bedroom.

Pete crossed the dim beige lobby into the white glare of the pharmacy. It smelled like perfumed medicine mixed with ammonia and rubbing alcohol. He could feel a familiar thirst on the back of his tongue. There were four people lined up at the prescription counter. He stood behind an elderly lady at the end of line. She was meticulous in her gray three-quarter-length cloth coat, dark caramel nylons, and black vinyl boots. She smelled like mothballs and damp wool. He stared at the prescription paper, but nothing sensible formed out of it. The elderly lady turned and glanced at Pete.

"Pardon me. Are you by any chance Peter Leonard?" she asked.

"Yes, I am."

"I am Donelda Peugot. I was your guidance counselor back at Waverly High."

"Mrs. Peugot, of course. I thought you looked familiar. It's been a long time."

"Many years. I barely recognize you anymore. You've changed a lot in thirty years. How are you? What are you doing these days?"

"Oh, I'm just getting along. I'm manager of the operations department in a technology services company."

"You always were so strong with technical subjects. You stand out in my memory as one of Waverly's most-likely-to-succeed students. You had a rare combination of technical aptitude, athletic talent, and social skills."

"Yeah, I guess I was lucky once. What brings you to the big city?"

"When my husband died, I moved here to be closer to my children and their families."

They chatted for a few more minutes. Pete rocked gently from side to side. The line still hadn't moved. He looked at his watch and then at the prescription. He excused himself, explaining that he had to get back to his office. Mrs. Peugot grasped his forearm with a wrinkled hand covered in light brown spots. "It was so nice to see you again, Peter. I hope life is treating you well and you've put many of your gifts to good use."

When Pete graduated from college with an advanced technology degree, he went to work for Newton-Millbank Tech Services. The company was just starting up, which made for exciting times. The company was growing, the industry was growing, and Pete was growing. His technical abilities quickly made him a troubleshooting star with NMTS's key customers. His easygoing manner made him popular inside and outside the company. He worked with the sales department to help close a couple of key accounts. Just a year after he started, he was promoted into his first management role. He loved it. Years of leadership on sports teams had given him strong instincts for rallying his group of techs to solve impossible problems under unreasonable deadlines.

It didn't take long for the industry to notice, and Pete's reputation and responsibilities grew. As his marriage to Chantal wilted, he spent more time at the office, increasing his profile. Throughout his thirties he moved to ever higher management levels while NMTS's growth exploded.

When both the market and the company slowed and stalled, work became work. Pete started to dread, and then resent, the numerous bosses who came with the continuous company reorganizations, and the unreasonable demands of both customers and the ungrateful people in his organization. Stress, anxiety, and irritability became his constant companions.

When they were thirty-three, he and Chantal divorced, with joint custody of the kids. Six years later Pete took the marital plunge again, this time with Michelle, a high-school drama teacher – who fortunately was not as dramatic as Chantal.

However, it wasn't long before he took his stress out on Michelle. Chantal's vitriolic barbs whenever they crossed paths while picking up or dropping off the kids didn't help much. He kept applying Chardonnay and beer to his nerves to keep himself sane. But lately, even increasing the dosages of these self-medications and throwing in extra-strength pain pills wasn't relieving his throbbing head.

Pete walked out the front door into the cold drizzle. Dark heavy clouds were sinking earthward from the dreary gray mass above. He zipped up his coat and raised his collar to shield himself from the sharp wind that was driving tiny wet needles into his face. He hurried across the front of the building toward the parking lot, catching a glimpse in the first-floor office windows of a fat, balding old man hunched over and shuffling sideways like a crab against the current. Poor old guy, he thought. Then he looked again and stopped dead. So did the old man. He stared at himself in the window. I sure could use a drink, he thought as he scurried to his car. He watched the pathetic old guy in the window try to straighten up and walk with dignity.

Once inside his car, Pete called to check his voice mail. The first message was marked urgent. He pressed the key to listen. He recognized the voice of his boss's assistant: "This is Rhonda Donald with a broadcast message for the client services management team. Mr. Drake is calling an emergency meeting tomorrow morning at nine in conference room two. Attendance is mandatory. Cancel whatever you have booked and be there." There was a click followed by the voice-mail lady declaring, "End of message."

Pete felt his heart pounding. Sighing, he deleted the message and started his car. The rain began pelting his windshield with a torrent of angry water.

The Call of the Riled

"So what's got Dougie's shorts in a knot this time?" Chuck asked, as the rest of the management team sat quietly around the conference table sipping their morning coffee. They were waiting for Doug and Rhonda to show up. They were late as usual.

Chuck headed up sales. He was tall and slim with a thick head of silver hair parted on the side and a graceful wave across his forehead. He'd been with NMTS for twenty-three years. He should have been feeling the heat of the company's current revenue crisis. But as he put it to Pete over a few beers the week before, "I am battle-weary and fed up with giving my life to this company. And I'm really sick of playing guess-what-Dougie-is-thinking. He just needs to tell me what he wants me to do and I'll do my best. I'm fifty-six and counting the days – seven hundred and forty-two to be exact – until I get my first pension check. Then my life will be my own again."

"But what if the company doesn't survive?" Pete had asked. "There may not be a pension for any of us if we keep playing the game by the old rules."

Chuck had waved his hand in contempt, dismissing even the possibility. "It will survive," he said. "You know Dougie well enough not to fall for his sky-is-falling BS. He's always trying to motivate us" – he made giant quotation marks in the air – "with his theatrical declarations of doom."

Now, in the conference room, Pete surveyed the rest of the management team's cast of characters.

Rosetta – everybody called her Rosie – was looking at the white face of the large clock on the conference room wall. "I wonder who decreed that every conference room in the world be painted the same drab shade of beige?" she said. "There must be entire paint factories running three shifts a day trying to keep up with demand. If NMTS made beige paint, we'd be in great shape. I'm going to take a wild guess and say the meeting today is about the latest numbers."

Rosie was in charge of the division's administrative department. She was short and plump with wiry hair in tight curls and a large pair of glasses that magnified her hazel eyes. Her frequent smile softened and lit up her round face. She looked like a friendly owl with frizzy head feathers. She'd been with NMTS for five years, after a short stint at a struggling start-up company. Her instincts were good. That company closed its doors for good two years later.

"Things do sound pretty grim," Harold added. "I hear the marketing budget is going to be trimmed back again. I don't think I can avoid showing some of my people the door. And they'll be the lucky ones. It's not like the workload is going to decrease." He looked across the table at Chuck. "I'm sure Doug will expect even more from us to fix our crumbling image and create more leads for your sales guys."

Harold was a fifteen-year marketing veteran of NMTS and now headed up the marketing department. He had the leathery face and husky voice of a heavy smoker. In baseball season he was very active as one of the region's top semi-professional league umpires. He rarely smiled anymore. Faded laugh lines, like traces of an old creek in a barren desert, hinted that humor once did visit his stern face. Harold no longer believed in a world of black and white, or good and bad. The constant pressure to perform had simply made everything either bleak or bleaker.

The rain didn't look like it was going to stop anytime soon. The wind was gusting and sheets of water washed against the second-floor conference-room window. The room was cold and musty. Somewhere in the distance water was faintly drip, drip, dripping at a constant and maddening tempo.

Rosie went to refill her coffee mug. Looking out the window, she sighed, "I heard this nasty weather is going to be with us for a few days."

"For every drop of rain that falls, a flower grows," Harold mused. "And a foundation leaks and a ball game gets rained out and a car rusts and ..."

Pete turned his attention to Omar, who had just joined the division two months earlier as head of Information Technology. He was new to the company. His easygoing and jovial manner nicely matched his rotund face and body. His shaved head showed the faint dark shadows of a hairline circling around the lower sides and back of his shiny skull. His brilliant white teeth contrasted with his light-brown complexion.

Damali was the division's head of accounting. She'd been with the organization for just over a year. Her straight black hair framed a slender tan-colored face of softly pock-marked skin. She liked to play the part of silent spectator.

"Morning," Doug barked as he threw open the door. Like a bad actor, he lived for the grand entrance. Rhonda was right behind him. As he made his way to the end of the table, everyone knew that today he was playing the part of a four-star general.

"Let's get right to it," he said.

Doug was of average height. His two most prominent features were his belly and his moustache. The former was perfectly rounded, as if he had a beach ball stuffed inside his mock turtleneck sweater. The latter was white, streaked with thin black stripes. It hid his upper lip and accentuated his large pink lower lip. His big fleshy face with its multiple chins and folds made him look more like a walrus than a general.

"We're in a deep %*#!* shit hole!" he declared as he pushed his glasses higher on his nose.

Doug believed that the strategic use of profanity shocked people into paying more attention. Pete thought he saw Chuck roll his eyes.

"Our sales are sliding off a cliff," Doug continued. "But our expenses are continuing to climb. We're running out of cash. So we need to restructure our finances. We need to come up with a plan showing we can turn this ship around and convince the banks to give us the credit we need until we do. Our job this morning is to figure out how to do that."

Pete reached into his pocket. He knew this was going to be a three-pill meeting.

"I'd like to start by understanding why our current results are so badly below forecast," Doug said, his moustache quivering slightly. "We're not even close to hitting our numbers."

Doug stared down the table at Chuck, who was sitting forward in his chair with his elbows on his knees. "Chuck, why are sales way off your projections?"

Chuck delivered his lines like a robot. "We're getting a lot of delayed decision making. It's partly due to customer concerns about our future viability and it doesn't help that we're at the low point of service-contract renewals right now. Our sales force is working flat out. There's some business in the pipeline that should close soon."

"Why don't I see projected sales of the new services we launched last quarter in your forecast reports?" Doug asked.

Pete remembered how Chuck had derided those new services as "Dougie's latest goofball idea for saving this company."

"We're just getting those valuable new services positioned to our prospects and customers now," Chuck said.

"So what's it going to take for your team to hit your numbers?" Doug asked.

"We need to see the market turn around and the press on this company to get better."

"Come on, Chuck! Are you telling me your sales plan is prayer? What specific steps are you taking to help us generate revenue today? If you can't tell me that, maybe I need to find someone who can."

Chuck studied his shoes. Everyone else became very interested in their notes, coffee mugs, or the water rivulets on the window. Rhonda's keyboard clacked as she recorded the meeting minutes on her computer.

"Getting stronger marketing support and fixing our service delivery issues would help too," Chuck said.

Harold scowled at Chuck and continued twisting a paper clip into new and unusual shapes.

Doug looked around the table. "Does anyone have a single new idea or insight?"

The hush said it all.

Finally, Omar spoke up. "As the new guy on the team, I'd like to offer some observations and suggestions," he said.

"Since IT gets deep into each department here, we get a good feeling for what's going on. I'm concerned by the large number of urgent projects and growing list of critical objectives we seem to have. It's overwhelming. We can't possibly do it all. On top of that, urgent new priorities seem to be thrown at us every day."

Mostly from the big guy at the head of this table, Pete wanted Omar to add.

"I think we need a better process for agreeing on our goals and priorities and sticking with them," Omar concluded.

Pete saw Chuck smirk and exchange a long look with Rosie. He tilted his chair backwards and crossed his legs. Like everyone else around the table, he knew the show was about to begin.

Doug glared at Omar. "We have a lot of urgencies because our situation is very urgent. Our biggest problem is lack of accountability. Managers here are not taking responsibility for delivering on what we agree to do. What do you suggest?"

Omar pulled a few stapled sheets from a file in front of him and handed one set to Doug. "I, I ... have made a list of the projects each department is working on that involves IT in some, in some, uh, way. As you can see, umm, it's an impossibly long list and there is a lot of overlap and duplication. So I have followed that with a master project-and-priority list based on my discussions with each department head."

Doug flipped through the first few sheets. He looked up and moved his big moustache upward and outward into what was intended to be a smile. "This is useful, Omar. Thank you. It's perfect timing for our budget review and the resetting of our strategies and plans."

Omar beamed. The rest of the group looked apprehensive.

In his best teacher-to-kindergarten-kid voice, Doug said, "Let's use this list to educate you, Omar, and highlight the lack of urgency and accountability problems we have in our division."

For the next hour and a half, he proceeded down the list, giving a forceful argument for the vital importance of every project. He grilled each manager on the ones that involved their groups. With each project he fiercely challenged the manager – or in some cases two or three managers – on whether they really thought this project should be moved off the top-priority list. No one did and none were.

When Doug pushed hard for an explanation of why a project was late or not completed, he was given quiet, mono-tone explanations, such as factors beyond the control of that group, how hard everyone was working on it, and how the project was being researched further. Doug would often interrupt with "that's unacceptable," "we can't keep delaying this project," "you really need to get on top of this."

It was a painful lesson for Omar to endure. His beaming face had faded to grim. Beads of sweat now formed above his eye brows and prepared to break out on his reddening forehead.

"So we agree that Omar's project list is valid," Doug said, looking around the table. "Omar, do you now understand how vital all of these projects are to dealing with our crisis?"

"Yes, I guess I do," was Omar's almost whispered response.

"Good. I'm glad we have a consensus on this one. Let's get the projects done, people, and damn all of your lousy excuses. Okay. We'll take a short break and then Heather is going to join our meeting to *enlighten* us with her report and recom-mendations regarding the organizational survey results in the client services division."

Doug and Rhonda left the room and went down the hall to Doug's corner office suite.

Omar got up and went to the men's room. Harold and Chuck followed him in. "So how do you like our management meetings so far?" Chuck asked with a cynical snicker as they stood beside each other at the urinals.

"It didn't go exactly as I'd planned," Omar replied. "I don't understand why you and the other managers didn't tell Doug what you were telling me about these projects. We can't do them all."

"Of course we can't," Harold said. "But it's a lot easier to get forgiveness than permission from Doug. We all just work on what are clearly the most important issues and tell him what he wants to hear."

"He's really easy to get along with once you learn to obey him," Chuck said. "And if he wants any of your bright ideas, he'll give them to you. Omar, you're a good guy and I am sorry to see you get grilled this morning. But I could spot this one coming a mile off when you pulled out your list."

By now Pete had joined in the proceedings. "Omar, we've all got battle scars from tangling with Doug. He figures that you're not carrying your share of the load if you don't have ulcers or marital problems. It's just easier to go along to get along with him."

Omar dried his hands, shook his head, and walked out the door back to the meeting room.

There was very little conversation around the table as the group waited ten minutes for Doug and Rhonda. When they finally marched in, Doug introduced Heather with barely disguised contempt as "having some corporate HR wisdom to share with us about this." He waved his copy of the organizational survey report with its dozens of little red Post-it Note flags flicking in the air.

Heather's presentation, complete with colorful bar and pie charts, was shown on the screen at the front of the meeting room. She was the corporate Human Resources director and not a member of the division's management team. Doug had grudgingly agreed to allow her into today's meeting when his boss, Cy Garnet, the company's president, had insisted she meet with the management team to review and interpret the organizational survey results that each manager had recently received.

Heather was in her thirties. She was about five feet two, slim, with straight shoulder-length auburn hair and a creamy smooth complexion. She radiated friendliness and approachability.

Running through the survey results, she pointed out how morale had dropped across the whole client services division, but especially Pete's operations department. The client services divisional results were lower, percentage-wise, than those of the overall company. She handled challenges to the validity and accuracy of the survey data, but most of the managers weren't convinced by her answers. The lowest categories were trust, communications, and teamwork.

Heather carried on: "In the past two weeks, I did further analysis of the written comments on the survey and talked with many people throughout your division to bring you some further insights on the management issues you might want to address. What's emerged is that people don't feel you're openly sharing information and letting them know what's really going on. But the biggest problem is the departmentalism and turf wars. Most of that seems to be a reflection of challenges this team has in working together."

Doug jumped on that comment and demanded examples. Heather measured her words carefully, describing e-mails that were circulating between marketing, sales, and operations with accusations and defenses flying back and forth. Doug had not heard of these contentious issues and demanded to be copied on the e-mails so he could "get to the bottom of this."

Pete grimaced. No doubt he'll fire out a succession of his infamous flaming e-mails to scorch us into being good little boys and girls, he thought.

Heather stated that a rising number of client service problems were because departments weren't keeping each other informed. Once again Doug demanded examples. Heather cited a few that would be almost funny if they weren't so damaging to internal and external relationships.

Chuck threw in that one had resulted in a medium-sized customer failing to renew its contract. He went on to complain about marketing's lack of urgency in meeting the sales department's needs.

Harold snapped back, "Failure to plan on your part should not make for an emergency on our part!"

Doug cut off further discussion.

The questions and discussions put Heather's portion of the meeting well into the lunch hour, and forty-five minutes past what seemed to be her allotted time. But since there was no posted agenda, no one was quite sure what Doug had in mind. Rhonda came to the rescue.

"Mr. Drake, you are late for your luncheon meeting," she said.

But Doug wasn't finished yet. "Thanks for your *enlightenment*, Heather," he said. His volume and pitch rose. "I am very disturbed by what I am hearing here. You have all got to get your act together and get along. If you can't start working together as a team, I may have to make some changes to get players who can."

With that he bounced to his feet and disappeared out the door. Rhonda snapped her computer shut, wrapped up the power cord, and followed in his wake.

Pete headed back to his own office. The voice-mail indicator light on his desk phone was flashing crimson red like an ambulance rushing to the scene of a horrific disaster. Probably a dozen messages, a bunch of them urgent, he thought. A glance at his computer screen showed forty-one new e-mail messages, many of them marked with red exclamation marks. This is exactly why I hate bloody meetings, he thought. He shook a few pills from the big plastic bottle in his desk drawer into his hand and poured his sixth or seventh coffee from his personal pot. Meetings get in the way of all the work we have to do around here. And this one was a huge waste of time when we can least afford it.

Pete sipped his coffee and stared out the window. He picked out individual raindrops slanting downward from the foggy mass overhead. On and on they fell, smash, smash, smashing into the clear wall. I know how that feels, he snorted to himself. He looked around the tight edges of the window. I'll bet these are sealed to keep us from jumping out.

Suddenly his eyes were drawn to a shadowy shape on the grass beside the parking lot below. Barely visible through the gloom was what looked like a large cow or horse nibbling on the lower branches of a small tree. It stopped and turned its head upward to gaze at Pete's office window. They locked eyes. Then it faded back into the mist.

I'm really losing it now, Pete thought, turning back to his computer.

The Dread POETS Society

"Hey Pete. A few of us are going for drinks after work," Rosie said as she stuck her frizzy head through the door to Pete's little office.

"After that inspiring meeting this morning, that's just the sort of action plan I can get behind," Pete said.

"Rocky and Bullwinkle's?"

"Perfect. I'll see you in an hour."

Rocky and Bullwinkle's was your typical roadhouse/restaurant/bar. It was just down the street from NMTS. Its theme and interior were loosely based on the old Rocky and Bullwinkle cartoon series.

Harold, Rosie, and Damali were already seated at a back corner table when Pete got there. He was surprised to see Damali. She hadn't said anything at the morning meeting and didn't normally socialize outside the office. Everyone respected her brisk efficiency and cool competency – especially since she had so quickly cleaned up the accounting mess she had been hired to fix.

"... he's going to pull down the whole division if something isn't done," Damali was saying with a passion and frankness Pete hadn't realized she could muster. "If the division goes, the whole company is gone."

Harold moved aside and pushed back a chair for Pete. "We're chatting about our delightful leader and his latest trail of destruction," he said with a weary grin.

"He's really killing us. And it's pulling down the morale of the whole division," Damali said, staring right at Pete.

"Welcome to this week's POETS meeting, Pete," Rosie said. "We're just beginning to compose." Rosie called their after-work drinks the Piss-On-Everything-Till-Sunrise Society, or POETS, for short.

Harold loved worn-out clichés and aphorisms. "This morning's meeting was yet another triumphant installment in the continuing saga that is the leadership lunacy of NMTS," he said. "The one who blows his horn loudest is most often in the fog."

Damali looked at Pete. "The list of projects that came out this morning is unbelievable. I knew we had a lot on our plates, but I had no idea the list was soooo long. Did you?"

"Operations is involved in many of these projects, so I had a pretty good idea," Pete said. "But I didn't see the big picture until today."

"I remember when you used to sort through all the conflicting priorities to help our team set clear goals and plans, Pete," Harold said.

Before Doug arrived at NMTS as senior vice president, Harold reported to Pete.

"You need to bring some of that discipline to this team," Harold said.

"No thanks! I am not taking Doug on over this one. I have enough scars on my back from his hobnail boots ..."

"Did they have multi-color mirrors on them like in the Beatles song?" Rosie asked, trying to lighten things up a little.

"Remember the issue with the Henderson Industries account?" Pete asked. "I tried to help him out with some input, and what thanks did I get? My budget was cut and two of my key projects were derailed. It cost me a good chunk of my bonus that year. I got the message. So, no thanks! Right now I need to save what's left of my sanity."

"We can't go on like this," Damali said. "It's the tyranny of the urgent. I can't stand the endless fire storms of crisis much longer. My department is burning out, and I am afraid we're going to lose some of our best people."

And you're one of them, Pete thought. If Damali left, it would be a huge loss to the division. He noticed red streaks radiating from the pupils of her eyes. He had never seen her looking so tired and distraught.

"The project list needs to at least be sorted into critically urgent, extremely urgent, and really urgent," Rosie said.

"Years back I would have thought for sure you'd be in Doug's SVP role by now," Harold said, gazing across his Coke at Pete.

Pete took a deep draught of beer. This is what he really needed to calm his jangled nerves. "Shoulda. Woulda. Coulda. Things just didn't work out," was his weak reply.

Chuck and Omar arrived and pulled chairs over to the table. "I thought today's victim could use a drink and the con-solation of the POETS Society," Chuck laughed, patting Omar on the back. Omar could only manage a rueful smile.

"This morning reminded me of the scene in the Roman senate when the dictator Sulla asked for any objections to his proposal," Chuck went on. "Ofella spoke up in opposition to Sulla's plans. Without saying a word, Sulla motioned to his henchmen waiting at the doors. They carried Ofella out to the courtyard and sliced off his head. Sulla then turned back to the senate and asked, 'Are there any other comments?' That pretty much took care of it. There was no further opposition from the floor."

One of Chuck's interests was ancient Roman history. Pete was sure it made him very popular at parties.

Damali offered sympathetic words to Omar on his initiation into the toxic culture of client services. She had an animated discussion with him about how deadly the atmosphere was in the division and just how critical his attempt to prioritize all the projects really was.

Chuck tried to comfort him too, saying, "Don't worry, Omar – I'll tell you some stories that will make you feel as if Dougie gave you a big hug and kiss this morning."

"What we've all learned is how useless it is to try what you did this morning," Rosie said. "There's no point. So you just go along – and then you meet with your fellow POETS to straighten out the world. Welcome to the society." She raised her glass to toast Omar.

"But he told me when I was hired that his style was all about consulting with his management team," Omar said. "He has emphasized that over and over in the few months I've been here. His e-mail to us last week mentioned getting our input and ideas to deal with our big problems. I thought I was providing that this morning."

"Doug talks a good game and can spout most of the latest management book leader-speak," Rosie said. "But his idea of consulting us is to get our agreement on a course of action that he's already decided on. He browbeats us into silence and takes that as agreement. When he asks for honest feedback, he's really telling you to agree with him. He's especially good at kissing up to those above him and kicking down those below. Welcome to the lower decks, my fellow POET."

As conversation continued at the other end of the table, Harold leaned over to Pete and asked, "So why aren't you sitting in Doug's chair? You had it all going for you."

"I don't know. I guess after all I'd been through with Chantal, I just ran out of gas."

"We could really use the old Pete Leonard, you know. You're the best one to deal with Doug and get us out of this jam. You have a long history and a lot of respect in this company. And I'm not just talking about this team. Cy Garnet is a big fan too."

Pete drained the last drops from his second pint. The familiar buzz didn't seem to strengthen him this time. "Cy would never undermine or override Doug," he said. "That would be the same as firing him. And as I said earlier, I am not about to try and take on Doug – especially given the warpath he's marching down these days."

"Pete, you've beat tough challenges before. Remember when you led our team through the impossible deadlines and corporate interference to deliver SCORPIO on time?"

Pete always smiled when he thought of how exhilarated and triumphant he felt the day SCORPIO – an innovative new client service plan – was presented at the annual general meeting. It was a stunning success by any standard and became one of the key contributors to NMTS's steep growth curve.

"We go back far enough together for me to know just what leadership you're capable of," Harold said. "I don't know how you've lost your way. I'm going to tell you this as a friend as much as a colleague, but it's disappointing to see you in this state. For your own sake and ours, you've got to get back on track."

"I'm not that guy anymore," Pete mumbled. "Now I am just going along to get along. If we lie low long enough, this too shall pass. Assuming the company makes it through this rough patch – and that I do too – I've got about seven or eight more years until my pension kicks in. I'll still be young enough to move on and do what I really want to do. The truth is, I can't afford to do anything at this point to jeopardize my job."

Pete recalled a tense discussion with Michelle a few nights earlier after she read that day's newspaper story about NMTS's prospects.

"My teaching job is very secure, so there's no worry about that income," she had said. "But we would be in a real mess if you lost your job right now. We have very little money saved and still have this house to pay for. Since you're getting close to fifty, you could have problems getting another job that pays as well as this one. And you wouldn't have much of a pension, so you'd have to keep working for many more years. I am not sure your health could take that."

Countless coffees at the office and a growing collection of empty pint glasses were catching up to Pete. Now the only relief he cared about was twenty steps away, in the men's room. He excused himself and dragged his feet slowly in that direction. He felt the prescription in his shirt pocket. Maybe I should stop at the drugstore and get this filled, he thought – or maybe it's time for another self-medicating pint. As he shuffled through the dim bar, he looked through the window and saw another torrent of rain soak the parking lot. Just then he remembered his umbrella. It was in the front seat of his car.

When Pete got back to the table, the conversation had turned to the organizational survey results. Everyone agreed that today's declining work values and unrealistic expectations from many of the new workers was a big part of the problem. The increasing turnover within client services was bringing many new people into the organization. They were just too unreasonable.

"What really frustrates me is their lack of initiative," Rosie said. "They seem to be constantly coming to me looking for direction. So I have to spend a big part of my day babysitting."

"I was surprised by the low scores – and some of the written comments were just downright cruel," Damali said. "If they feel so strongly about some of these issues, why don't they speak up? It's actually a bit cowardly not to tell us directly what their gripes are."

"And don't they love to bitch and moan when they're together?" Chuck said. "They should put up or shut up. The other day I overheard a couple of staff whining about a problem with another department. So I suggested they bring it forward to that group and do some problem solving with them. They told me there's no point because the other group isn't going to change anyway. Of course they won't change if you don't take some initiative to address the issues with them."

The group continued, over yet another round of drinks, to bitterly denounce their weak staff, Doug, demanding customers, market conditions, and fierce competition.

"I am beginning to think that our luck is so bad that if NMTS went into the cemetery business, people would stop dying," Damali said.

"Well, I am feeling better now that us POETS have given up all hope," Rosie said with a laugh.

"After this morning's meeting, I can see that NMTS's office is really hell with fluorescent lighting," Omar said. Rosie congratulated him on his poetic observation and knighted him with her straw, making him an official member of the POETS Society.

Harold contributed another saying. "In our division if you stoop you'll be stepped on and if you stand tall you'll have your head lopped off and handed to you by Doug."

"Cheer up. The whole world isn't against us," Chuck said. "I think I know of some people and smaller countries that don't care."

Rosie looked at her watch. "*Oh my god*, look at the time! I've got to get going." She put on her coat while others began to get up from the table. "Thanks for the misery of your company," she said and headed for the door.

"I am glad I joined you today," Damali said to the rest of the group. "This conversation has confirmed what I was feeling, and now I know what I need to do to preserve my sanity."

Pete didn't like the sound of that at all. He was just finishing the last of yet another beer when Heather walked over to the table. "Hi guys. Looks like I missed the party," she said. "I wanted to join you earlier, but I got tied up at the office reviewing the survey with Doug."

"I'm sure *that* was an inspiring time," Pete said.

Harold pulled up a chair for her. "I was just about to mention Jason Reynard's upcoming workshop to Pete," he said. "Since you circulated the e-mail about it, you're just the person to sell him on attending. I heard Jason speak a few years back at a conference. He's got some good things to say on leadership that I think Pete would find helpful. I've been trying to wake up the old Pete Leonard that I know is still hiding inside that body somewhere. We could really use his leadership these days."

"I have heard a few of the impressive stories about your key contributions to NMTS's early success," Heather said to Pete. "I think you would find Jason's workshop very helpful. I attended one of his public workshops a few months ago and

I've read a couple of his leadership books. He's very good and his advice is quite practical. Would you be interested in attending?"

"I'm sure it would be beneficial, but I just can't get away for a whole day right now," Pete said. "Besides, Doug would be on my case about that too. He doesn't believe in soft stuff like leadership training."

"True," Heather said. "He isn't exactly enthusiastic about the workshop. But with Cy's insistence, he's supporting it. It's great timing to help you get some ideas for leadership improvement around the survey results."

They talked about the workshop and some of Jason's leadership principles over another round of drinks. Harold and Heather continued to encourage Pete to attend. He continued to insist that he was too busy. He was beginning to slur his words.

As they finished up, Harold said to Pete, "I've only had a few Cokes. Why don't you leave your car here and I'll drop you off at your place? It's not far out of my way."

Pete rose to his feet. He felt dizzy. "Yeah, I guess I did overindulge a little. Maybe that's not a bad idea. Thanks."

It was now totally dark. Harold's car sliced through wisps of mist and moved in and out of thickening fog. As they were turning down the road leading into his subdivision, Pete noticed a large four-legged shadow up ahead. It stepped off the grassy boulevard right onto the road. As they sped closer, Pete peered through mist and realized it was the cow or horse he had seen in the afternoon.

"Look out! We're going to hit it!" he shouted to Harold. That was the last thing he remembered as he raised his arms in front of his face and braced for impact.

Of Moose and Managers

Coffee cup in hand, Pete quietly slipped into one of the few empty seats at the back of the conference room. He nodded at his neighbor as he sat down, splashing coffee on the white tablecloth. That's about par for me, he thought, watching the brown stain spread across the table.

He had stopped by the office on the way to the session. He should have known better. Most mornings he felt like a fire chief struggling to get the latest blaze under control, and today was no different. Then traffic was heavy due to the continuing rainy weather and a serious car crash.

Jason Reynard was well into reviewing the day's agenda with a colorful slide showing on a large screen to his right. He looked to be in his mid-fifties, with receding gray hair. He was fairly fit and trim. He had a friendly, low-key style that was also animated and energetic. His quips and comments were drawing laughter from around the room as people settled in. There were about twenty tables with about half a dozen participants at each.

Jason was now talking about workshop expectations. "I am going to be giving you a fire hose of ideas today. You can drink deeply from the fire hose, you can gargle, or you can just rinse and spit." He asked participants to spend a few minutes jotting down what they wanted to take away from the session in their personal workbooks.

Pete stared at the blank page with "Workshop Objectives" at the top. He didn't really have any expectations because he knew he was wasting precious time being there while new fires were starting back at the office.

Pete vaguely remembered coming to and finding himself sitting in Harold's car as it idled in his driveway. Harold was very worried about him – especially after Pete screamed to stop the car. Harold claimed he hadn't seen anything and that whatever Pete thought he saw was probably "ale induced." Pete couldn't remember much more about their conversation except for Harold's worried tone and deep concern for "the slippery slope you seem to be on."

A day later, Doug called Pete to his office and told him that he was registered to take Jason Reynard's one-day leadership workshop the following week. "It's to help you get your act together and get things turned around in operations," he said gruffly.

Pete protested that he didn't have time for it. Doug agreed that the timing was bad, but said maybe Pete would pick up a few things that would make it worthwhile. He told Pete to get the workshop registration package from Rhonda on his way out. He was dismissed. Later, Pete learned that Harold had had a long conversation with Heather about his concerns. She had apparently talked to Cy, who in turn had spoken to Doug. And so here he was this morning.

The six people around Pete's table introduced themselves. They were managers and supervisors from a cross-section of organizations. Each then talked about why they were here and their expectations for the day. Pete wasn't that keen to participate, so he danced around his expectations and didn't join any further discussion.

A few minutes later, Jason summarized on a flip chart at the front of the room the numerous workshop expectations he was given. Then he said, "A key theme of today's session is courageous leadership. That's having the courage to navigate change we don't want. It's having the courage to strengthen our leadership in the face of daily management crises and technical issues pulling us down into the minutiae of details. It is especially about having courageous conversations. That means having the courage to talk about sensitive issues we've been avoiding and having the courage to listen to what we don't want to hear."

As Jason carried on along these lines, Pete discreetly checked his e-mail and typed a few quick replies about yet another burning issue.

When he tuned back into the meeting, Jason was saying, "Poor time management and overwork – too many e-mails, voice mails, and meetings – are often the result of not enough courage to face issues – either at work or even at home. So we avoid them by burying ourselves in our busyness. For many less-effective managers, volumes of e-mails, voice mails, phone calls, and meetings are a twisted type of status symbol or personal measure of self-worth proving to them and others just how busy, important, and indispensable they are."

Spoken like a theoretical consultant who's never had to manage a demanding organization, Pete thought as he tapped out another e-mail.

Now Jason was talking about dealing with adversity. "I used to mouth the phrase 'embrace change.' In the last few years I have changed my perspective on change. Now I believe that 'embrace change' is a useless platitude uttered by someone who's either never really thought about its full implications or is a masochist. Many changes are impossible to embrace. This list might include loss of a relationship, a loved one, health, job, money, and such."

Pete stopped answering the e-mail. Now the guy is finally making some sense, he thought.

"We may not choose the adverse changes that spring up," Jason said. "But we always choose how we respond."

Jason went on to show a slide with a dotted line running horizontally across the middle of it. "This is Survivor mode. We're sitting on the fence to see what happens or passively waiting for someone else to do something. There are times when being an above-the-line Survivor and not acting immediately is quite wise. This might be when we need more information and have to do some research, or to see whether a change is going become a trend, or which way the new boss, government, etc. is going to go."

Then he showed a slide with "Navigator" written well above the line from the previous slide. "When we're in Navigator mode, we're trying to capitalize on the problem or adversity. Or we may be at least trying to figure out how we can make the best of a bad situation. This section above the line is leadership territory. Like the best ship captains of old, strong or courageous leaders know that we can't control the wind and currents, but we can adjust our sails to make the best use of the conditions to move toward our destination."

He then moved to a slide with the word "Victim" well below the line. "In Victim mode we're bitter, helpless, and feeling like 'they' are doing it to us. In your world, who is 'they'?"

Participants answered with "the government," "my boss or senior management," "other departments," "customers," "workers," and "competition."

"These problems can be making our life difficult, but what matters is how we frame them," Jason said. "Courageous leaders face these issues head-on by focusing on what's within their direct control or influence. They figure out how to let go of, or at least not 'awfulize' and give more power to problems or issues that can't be controlled or changed. Leaders know that the best thing to do when it's raining, is to … let it rain. So leaders get busy figuring out how to work in the rain or adjust their sails rather than cursing the weather and moving to Pity City. Maybe you know a few people who live there?"

"Live there! My husband's the mayor," a woman at a front table said. "He runs the place!" A roar of laughter filled the room.

"Pity City – or its suburb, Frown Town – can be a therapeutic place to visit occasionally. We all need to grieve or ventilate our frustration when faced with major losses or setbacks. But we don't want to take up residence in this toxic place. Residency leads to deepening cynicism, despair, and inaction. It's certainly not leadership territory. But it's so easy to get on the Bitter Bus rolling on down Helpless Highway to Pity City because that's where so many people are going."

Jason acknowledged the groans emanating from the tables. "Okay, okay. But it takes much more courage and effort to fight against the natural gravity that is pulling us down and climb back up above the line. A popular party pastime is playing The Blame Game. Like that old 1960s game Twister, this game involves getting bent out of shape as we avoid taking any responsibility and denounce everyone else for the state of our affairs."

He went on to show a number of statistics and studies on

the deadly health effects of living below the line. They included dramatically increased rates of heart attacks, strokes, cancer, and depression. Pete thought of his visit to Dr. Yantzi's and the prescription for antidepressants he still had in his wallet.

"Life isn't fair. Lots of unfair and unjust crap happens to undeserving people," Jason was saying. "Whatever hits the fan won't be evenly distributed. But it's our choice whether to stand in it or not."

Jason took a blue marker and shaded in a large heavy dot on a clean flip-chart page. He then talked about how we can narrowly focus on just the dot by restricting our field of vision to this problem and ignoring the rest of the page. To demonstrate this further, he formed a circle with his index finger and thumb and placed it over his eye, thrusting his face right up to the dot on the page.

"In Victim mode, I can easily frame a problem so narrowly that it's all I can see," he said. "I lose perspective and can't see the huge amount of good or positive factors of all the white space on the rest of this page."

When he pulled back from the flip chart and looked back at the audience, he was greeted with hearty laughter. He hadn't realized that his marker was leaking and blue ink was all over the side of his index finger. He had left a large spot of ink beside his right eye. A participant at the front table offered him a moist cloth to clean himself up.

Jason tried to continue with his point about how our focus becomes our reality, but drew more laughter when his attempts to wipe off the spot smeared the blue ink all around his upper cheek beside and under his eye. Someone else gave him a mirror, moist wipes, and paper napkins. He reduced the ink somewhat, but a large blue stain remained on the side of his face. Someone at Pete's table said, "I guess this really shows how when we get overly focused on a problem we can't see much else. In a couple of minutes he's gone from having a problem to being really blue." There were a few nods of agreement and groans at the pun.

Jason reviewed his Navigator-Survivor-Victim chart. "Navigators make it happen," he said. "Survivors watch it happen. Victims ask, 'Why does this always happen to me?'"

During his table's brief discussion of this chart, the woman beside Pete reflected on the team she was leading. "We aren't always on the Bitter Bus," she said. "But we're often at the front of the line at the bus stop because if that's where our organization is going, we want to get a good seat."

Jason concluded this section of the agenda by showing a slide with an optical illusion on it. Two large red dots were surrounded by white frames. However, one frame was very thick and heavy and the other was small and thin. This made the dots look different sizes.

"Life is an optical illusion," he said. "We don't see the world as it is. We see the world as we are. Our perspective becomes our life."

Oh isn't that a lovely idea, Pete thought. He's telling me my attitude is to blame for all the crap in my life. Just put on a happy face and use good old positive thinking and my problems will all disappear? Yeah, right.

The rest of the morning passed quickly. Pete found the discussion interesting on many levels. He was really surprised to realize that he hadn't checked his e-mail in over an hour. He never thought he'd actually find anything worth listening to at the workshop and definitely wasn't prepared to find himself vigorously participating in the table discussions.

After lunch Jason began the afternoon session by announcing, "Now we're going to deal with courageous conversations by discussing Moose on the Table. This is where everyone in a meeting knows there is an issue or problem, but no one is talking about it. It's like there is a large moose standing on the meeting-room table and no one is saying a word about it, as if it's not there. The problem is that the longer the moose is ignored, the bigger it grows. Then it's joined by other moose attracted to the conspiracy of silence – the perfect habitat for these moose to thrive. And they start to have babies. Pretty soon moose are everywhere as everyone does their best to ignore them."

One participant near the front of the room observed that she had heard this phenomenon referred to as "elephant in the room." Jason agreed that it was the same idea.

"The consequences of not having courageous conversations that identify and address Moose on the Table can be quite serious. A major pulp and paper producer had a chemical cleaning procedure that was not being followed properly at one of its facilities. A worker raised it twice with management and was ignored. So he reported the environmental violations and spills to the government. They investigated and levied a ten-million-dollar fine and put two managers in prison for three years. The supervisor's defense was the ever-popular and cowardly cop-out – 'we always did it that way.'"

Jason went on to give a few more dramatic examples of how silence killed organizations – or even literally killed people when safety issues weren't addressed. "When moose run wild in an organization, it leads to a myriad of problems," he said. "Some of the more common ones are listed in your workbook."

Pete turned to the page and read through the list:

1. *Hiding/suppressing information*
2. *Minimizing or avoiding big problems/issues*
3. *Learned helplessness, cynicism, and apathy*

4. *Turf protection and silos or departmentalism*
5. *Team members dislike and avoid each other*
6. *Blame storming, fault finding, and sniping (often wrapped in "humorous" zingers)*
7. *Lower respect for self and others*
8. *Mediocre meetings*
   - *Mainly progress reports and updates*
   - *No real discussion, debate, or dialogue*
   - *Too much time focused **in** and not enough **on** the business*
   - *A few people dominate while the rest are spectators*
   - *Confusion between Command, Consultation, or Consensus decision making on each agenda item*
   - *Meetings lack clear agendas, strong facilitation, ground rules, conflict resolution, regular summaries of decisions/ progress, clear action planning, and follow-through*
9. *Messengers are shot and wounded, never to make that mistake again*
10. *Lobbying, politicking, and decision making are done outside the meeting*
11. *The boss makes decisions, then uses meetings to "hold court" or "discuss" what's happening*
12. *"Are there any questions?" is really a dare from a boss to say anything that's considered to be disagreeable*

Yep. NMTS has got pretty much most of those covered, Pete thought. Especially points 2, 4, 8, 9, and 11.

"What keeps us from having courageous conversations?" Jason asked.

"Fear," replied a thirty-something participant at the table just in front of Pete's.

"I agree," Jason said. "Take a few minutes at your table to discuss what sort of fear holds you back from talking about issues you know you need to address."

Everyone at Pete's table looked at each other without speaking. Finally an older man across from Pete said, "As I look back on my career, one of my biggest regrets is that I talked about the moose out in the hallway or with a few colleagues in our offices after meetings. But I didn't have the courage to raise the issue in the meetings when it really needed to be discussed. I guess I excused myself by rationalizing that I didn't want to rock the boat and jeopardize my job or promotion."

The man, feeling the support of the group, continued. "The financial pressure of raising kids, mortgages, and pursuing an ever higher lifestyle put me on a path that reduced my options and slowly silenced me into just going along. I didn't think that I could afford to speak up and live according to my true values."

He paused to gather his thoughts. "I see now that it's far too easy to let our courage ebb as the tide of responsibility rises. I lost my passion and settled for the status quo. So I ended up sedating my youthful ideals with booze, pills, and busyness."

Whoa! This guy is pretty pathetic, Pete thought. Life is about compromise. That's why it's better to keep your expectations low so you won't end up full of regrets like this gloomy old chap.

A couple of others at the table commented that he was being far too hard on himself.

"That might be true," the man said, "but with few working years left, there isn't a lot of time to develop the courage and approaches it takes to start acting like a leader. Now is the time for me to start changing the next five years. I am determined to finish my career by speaking up and speaking out."

Jason asked the group how people were punished for naming the moose in their organizations. Many participants were keen to share their experiences and perspectives. Responses included being suddenly excluded; branded as not a team player; anger or irritation from the boss or peers; put downs – often disguised as humor; reassignment to less-important roles or projects; not being promoted or taken off the fast track; and even being fired or "downsized."

"Good organizations confront brutal facts and weak ones avoid them," Jason said. "Avoiding moose issues is short-term gain for long-term pain. Courageous leaders navigate above the line and find ways to contribute to authentic conversations to address the moose. Cowardly leaders feel victimized by the moose and powerless to do anything, because they live below the line."

He paused, stood square to his audience, and asked, "How do you live with yourself, perpetuating a lie and not having honest conversations?"

No one replied. Pete felt that Jason was looking directly at him.

"I am challenging you to find the courage to live above the line," Jason said. "Be a Navigator. Be a moose hunter. Be a leader."

The old man at Pete's table turned around to look at the rest of the table, bobbing his head up and down in agreement.

As the workshop concluded, Pete gave it a rating on the feedback form of three on a five-point scale. Jason did have some good points to make and was a very skilled presenter, Pete thought, but his advice was unrealistic for his situation. He left the room quickly to avoid talking to anyone else. He wanted to get back to the office to deal with some of his most pressing concerns.

By the time he got to the office, through especially heavy rush-hour traffic, the building was deserted. A good time to try and catch up a little, Pete thought, as he took the elevator to the second floor. Just as he stepped out of the elevator, he heard heavy clomping and running noises. This was accompanied by a loud snorting sound.

"Look out!" a man's voice yelled. Pete caught a blur of brown in the corner of his left eye just as somebody smashed into him and flung him toward the far wall. His head hit a small table holding a vase of dried flowers. Then everything went black.

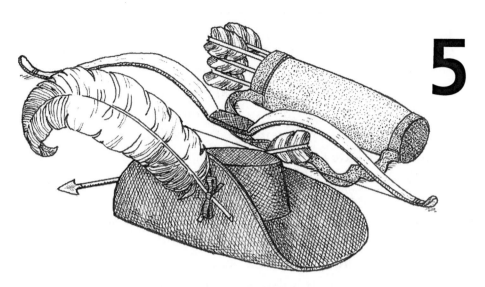

5

Elf Perception

"Who are you and what do you want with me?" Pete asked. His mind was fuzzy and it felt like all his senses were masked with gauze. Was it a concussion, he wondered, before forcing himself back to the more immediate problem of the stranger in front of him. "Are you robbing us?"

"No, no. Not at all," the stranger replied as if offended by the mere suspicion of wrongdoing. "I am Alfred, and I have come to protect you."

"Protect me?"

"Yes. I've come to protect you from the elk."

"Elk?"

"I suppose you call them moose in these parts," Alfred offered with a questioning look. Pete didn't respond.

"They're taking over your office, you know, and they can be very dangerous."

"Moose?" Pete replied groggily. "Dangerous?"

As his vision cleared, Pete got his first real look at Alfred. He had a light blond moustache hiding under a long pointed nose. His sideburns ran from the side of his hairline to the tip of his chin in a one-inch strip, following the contours of his sharp, bony face. He wore a large black broad-rimmed hat that would have been round if he hadn't pinned the right side back. A plume of black-and-white feathers was pinned to the underside of the raised portion, sweeping back a foot above and behind him. The feathers quivered whenever he moved his head. He was wearing a sleeveless cloth vest with elaborate designs cut into the breasts, back, and along the rounded panels defining its waist. What could best be described as a puffy purple fabric made up what Pete supposed was a shirt – although it was only the sleeves protruding through the wide brown flaps that winged each shoulder of the vest. Dark stockings and tanned leather boots completed the outfit. The brown leather strap running diagonally across his chest held a quiver of arrows on his back. A large bow was leaning against the wall.

Pete was positive he had just sustained the worst concussion in history. And what was the best his injured brain could come up with? Robin Hood. Bloody great.

He continued to lie on the coarse carpet of the small conference room. Alfred knelt down beside him, wiping blood off his forehead with a green handkerchief. "Let me get you some water," he whispered. He went over to the water cooler and filled the cheap plastic cup to the brim. Heading back to Pete, he stumbled on the carpet. If Pete wasn't fully awake before, ice-cold water in the face certainly did the trick.

"Sorry, sorry, sorry," Alfred stage-whispered, as he dried Pete's face with the handkerchief and attempted to dab some of the water from his soaking shirt.

"Why are you whisp—" Pete was cut off when Alfred quickly put his hand over his mouth.

"The big bull might hear us and charge right through that flimsy door. Elk can hear pretty well."

Pete still wasn't sure he was truly in this surreal scene with this bizarre character whispering in his ear.

"He almost got me just as you came off the elevator," Alfred said. "He knows I'm a threat to him and the cows he's courting in this office." Alfred's tone grew urgent. "We should get out of here. Are you feeling well enough to head downstairs?"

Pete nodded his head.

"You'll need to wear these to see the elk, I mean, moose."

Alfred pulled a pair of glasses with heavy black frames from his vest pocket. Pete put them on. They didn't seem to change his vision at all.

Alfred crept to the door, slowly. He opened it and stuck his head into the hallway, quickly twisting it from side to side. He motioned Pete to follow him. Pete rose to his knees. A sudden wave of nausea passed over him. He took hold of the conference-room table and got to his feet. I could really use a couple of stress beans right now, he thought.

Alfred grasped his huge bow and inched cautiously out into the hall, with Pete stumbling behind him. As he passed through the door to the stairwell, a huge bull moose rounded the corner on the other side of the elevators. It lowered its great rack of antlers and started to charge.

"Come on!" Alfred grabbed Pete's arm with surprising strength and pulled him through the stairwell door. In his rush to shut the door on the moose, he slammed it on Pete's arm. Pete almost fainted from the pain but managed to pull his arm through the door just as he felt the bull's antlers brush by.

They ran down the stairs and burst out into the front lobby. "Let's sit over here for a minute," Alfred said, pointing to a couple of overstuffed chairs. Pete dropped into the closest one and took a few moments to catch his breath. His arm throbbed and his forehead ached. Alfred went to sit on the chair's arm, but misjudged and nearly fell to the floor. His bow flew from his hand and spun across the shiny fake marble floor.

"Who are you and what the hell is going on?" Pete asked. "If you're a hallucination, I'd like to trade you in for another model. Preferably without the tights and cutesy outfit."

"I am your guardian elf, and I've been sent here help you deal with your moose problem."

"What an amazing coincidence. Until you arrived, we didn't have a moose problem."

"Actually you've been gradually building toward the major moose infestation you now have. The longer you ignore it, the harder it will be to get the problem under control."

"Well, I never saw any moose before you gave me these godawful ugly glasses."

"What about the moose outside your office window and the one you and Harold almost hit on the way home from the bar?"

"Those were just figments of my imagination ... Hey! How did you know about those? Unless you're also a really bad figment of my stressed-out imagination – or a bad dream I'm stuck in."

"Unfortunately for me, I'm not a figment of your very limited imagination. And I've been forced to learn much more about you and your pathetic life than I ever wanted to know. You have got to be the biggest coward I've ever seen. You wouldn't last a week where I come from."

"And if you don't come from my own mixed-up mind, then just where do you come from?"

"From a long line of English hunters. Elk – or what are called moose in North America – are our main prey." He walked over and picked up his longbow.

"So why is there suddenly a bull moose terrorizing our office?" Pete asked.

"There's nothing sudden about his appearance. That moose has been battling with another bull over the cow moose growing up in every office and cubicle in your company. It's grown to be quite the herd."

"Where do they come from, and why can't we see them?"

"We're still trying to figure some of that out. The moose seem to thrive in environments where people have real issues communicating with each other and spend a lot of time dodging problems they know have to be resolved. The more the issues are ignored, the bigger the moose grow. The hunters in our band appear to be the only ones who can see them without the special glasses I gave you. Although I do have to say that Jason Reynard did a good job in today's workshop of describing what seems to be happening."

"Stupid metaphor," Pete said.

"Well, you *met a four* ... legged ... animal ..." Alfred paused for effect. When Pete ignored the bad pun, he continued, "That was pretty real tonight, didn't you think? What we don't understand is why we're not able to shoot these moose. I've tried a few times, but my arrows pass right through them."

"So they're not real!"

"Oh they're real. I still have a nasty scab on my butt from the last time I got the sharp end of your metaphor. I tripped trying to get away from the other bull in your office." Alfred stood up. "Do you want to see it?"

"No!" Just then Pete noticed the night janitor drive his truck up to the front door. "That's all I need," he said. "Word getting out that I got caught in the lobby with some nutcase with his tights around his ankles."

Alfred followed Peter's gaze to the janitor. "You're the only one who can see me. He'd have no idea what you're looking at or who you're talking to."

"Oh, that's sooo much better. I'm sitting in the lobby talking to myself."

Pete quickly pulled out his phone earpiece and fitted it around his ear.

"Good evening, Mr. Leonard," the janitor called out as he came into the lobby.

Pete waved, pointed to the earpiece, and bobbed his head as if listening to someone on the other end of the phone call. The janitor waved back and nodded, then headed for the elevator.

"Impressive. That was quicker thinking than I've come to expect from you," Alfred said, after retrieving his bow. As he turned to face Pete, his longbow swung around behind him, knocking the glasses off Pete's face and poking him in the eye. Pete yelped and nearly fell out of his chair. Alfred rushed over to see if he was okay.

"Stay away from me, you clumsy idiot! I'll be fine if you just get out of my life." His eye stung and his sight was blurry. He rocked in his chair, holding his eye with both hands. "Guardian elf, my ass! You're a purveyor of pain. The custodian of calamity."

"That doesn't do much for my elf-confidence," Alfred said. "Besides, I'm the one getting the truly crappy part of this deal. I'm stuck trying to help a coward like you live up to your name. In fact, you're a mockery to every Leonard who's come before you."

"What are you talking about?" Pete said. The pain was easing from excruciating sharp stabs to dull thuds pounding against his eyelids.

"Your last name – Leonard – means 'brave lion' in English. It's derived from the Germanic element 'leon' or 'lion,' combined with 'hardy.' But you're about the farthest thing from brave or hardy I can imagine."

"Why do you say that?"

"Look at your life, Pete! You're a walking wonder of nature: a spineless creature who can still manage to stand upright. Well, almost upright," Alfred said, looking at Pete's drooping shoulders. "What about that meeting last week? There were moose standing on the meeting-room table. But you all chose to ignore them. That just makes them bigger and bolder. Why didn't you stand up to your bully boss?"

Alfred paused and shook his head. "Then a couple of you slunk into the men's room and talked about how you really felt. You all knew Omar was right, yet you let him swing from the antlers of the biggest moose in the room. That's the kind of cowardly behavior moose love."

By now Alfred had retrieved Pete's glasses. "Did you know that the word 'moose' comes from the Algonquian natives here in North America? It's derived from their word 'mons' or 'moz' – depending on the dialect. The loose translation is 'twig eater,' because they browse on tips of twigs, especially recent growth."

Alfred handed Pete his glasses. "Unresolved issues that aren't discussed are providing lots of new twigs for them to graze on in your office. And we've noticed that cowardly e-mails – where people say things they won't say in person – seem to provide especially good forage for them."

"Screw courage! I want to keep my job," Pete said. "You're being way too harsh. We all have mortgages to pay and pensions to protect. That's something you obviously don't understand."

"What I don't understand is why you don't speak up and deal with the moose. If you coast along to retirement without addressing the issues, then what? How will you feel about yourself? Is that all there is to life – getting by? You're no Leonard; you're a cowardly lion."

Alfred pointed to their reflection in the rain-streaked lobby window. "Fifteen years ago, is that the Peter Leonard you expected to be looking at today?"

Pete saw an overweight old man with rounded shoulders slumped in a chair. He ached all over. The familiar vice was squeezing his head. I could sure use a drink, he thought. He turned away and reached into his pocket for some pain relief. He shook a few of the comforting pills into his hand.

Alfred dropped his longbow and leapt from the arm of his chair. In a quick, sweeping motion, he smashed the container and pills from Pete's hands. They spun across the lobby floor and banged up against a wastebasket. "You've got to stop using those coward pills and start dealing with your issues," he said. Then he ran over to the pill container and stomped on it a few times with his tan leather boots. The small plastic bottle split open, leaving left little piles of mashed white powder all around it.

Alfred strode back to Pete. "You can't keep taking pills to dull your pain. Your go-along-to-get-along philosophy is a disaster. If it doesn't literally kill you, it will suck out your soul and leave nothing but this revolting dead-man-walking shell behind."

Alfred gave Pete a hard and very painful punch to his left shoulder.

Great, Pete thought. Now he had a matching ache to his other arm.

"What is with you people?" Alfred shouted. "The pile of pills this society uses is unbelievable. Nobody seems to want to deal with the root causes of pain and unhappiness. You flock together and take comfort in numbers like a bunch of sheep. If a room full of cowardly people all say something cowardly, it's still cowardly."

Pete studied the floor as he rubbed his throbbing left shoulder. At that very second he knew exactly what was causing his pain and it looked a lot like a guy in tights.

Alfred flopped back into his chair with a loud sigh. "So after the meeting of the meek, there you were sedating yourself with alcohol in the middle of a Pity Party at Rocky and Bullwinkle's. A sadder bunch of spineless whiners I have never seen. You're all brave warriors when you're down the street huddled together over glasses of liquid courage. And you gutless complainers had the gall to criticize your *staff* for doing the same thing! Whose example do you think they were following? How can whiny weaklings be strong leaders for them?"

The chirp of Pete's phone ringer echoed through the lobby. It was Michelle. "Yes, the leadership workshop was interesting," he told her. "I was tied up longer than I expected at the office and am just heading home."

"I'll ride with you and we can talk some more," Alfred said as he gathered up his longbow and followed Pete to the front door.

"Oh that would be just super," Pete said. "I love being insulted and assaulted by you because it feels so good when you stop."

In his attempts to jam his longbow into the back seat of Pete's Honda, Alfred hit the back window on the driver's side so hard, Pete looked closely for a crack. He didn't find one. Alfred didn't seem to notice or care as he put his hat with the big black-and-white feather on the floor. Cold rain continued to fall as they drove out of the dim parking lot.

"So if the plural of mouse is mice, is the plural of moose meese?" Pete asked as he stopped at a red light.

"No, the plural of moose is actually moose. And the biggest moose of the herd hangs around your office. He has one of the largest racks of antlers and the biggest bell I've ever seen."

"What's a bell?"

"That's the flap of skin and long hair that hangs down from his throat. It seems to indicate male virility."

"Ah, I can just picture it now. Two moose cows are chewing twigs together and one says to the other, 'Hey, Ethel! Take a good look at the clapper on that burning hunk of moosehood!'"

The elf looked puzzled at this.

Obviously there was a reason he'd never heard of an elf doing stand-up comedy, Pete thought. "Oh, never mind, after tonight, I need a bit of levity to save me from going totally over the edge," he said.

"That driver is really staring at you," Alfred said nodding toward the window. "I think you'd better wear your talking ear thing again."

Pete pulled out and positioned his earpiece. "Honest, officer. I haven't had anything to drink. And I am not talking to myself. I have been chatting with my old buddy Alfred here. He's an ancient moose hunter that only I can see. He's come from god-knows-where to save me from a herd that's taking over my office right here in the middle of the city. Sounds believable, don't you think?"

Alfred reached over and gave Pete's nose a very hard flick. "You convinced me, big guy."

They drove in silence along the wet streets. Finally Pete turned to Alfred and asked, "Why is the biggest moose hanging around my office?"

"Because there are so many issues there to feed on. Since you've become such a big coward, you're too afraid to address them. So the moose knows he's safest there. In heraldry, a *lion couard* – or cowardly lion – was depicted with his tail between his legs. That's what you've turned the noble Leonard name into, cowardly Pete."

"Very educational. I'm just going to ignore your rude personal put downs."

"In keeping with your gutless character."

"What do I need to do to get rid of the moose?"

"To start with, you need to find the courage to listen to your own team. Despite your much-proclaimed open-door policy, everyone in your organization has stopped coming to you because you refuse to even acknowledge that the problems exist. Or you find creative ways to avoid them. Or worse still, you try to blame someone else. It's classic victim behavior. You used to navigate these things so well when you first came aboard the good ship NMTS. Now it's like you're going to sink if you make the slightest decision or take on any responsibility. And now the waters are flooding into your personal life."

"So what do I do?"

"I think you need to identify and address the biggest moose issues in your own team."

The windshield wipers kept a steady, hypnotic beat as Pete drove on. Just before he pulled onto his street, he asked, "So are you going to follow me into my house too?"

There was no response. The passenger seat was empty. Pete looked in the back seat. The longbow was gone. There was nothing on the floor mat where Alfred's hat had been.

Michelle had kept Pete's dinner warm for him – again. She tried to get the conversation going as he ate, but his mind was somewhere else. She finally gave up and left the table. Pete hardly noticed that she was gone.

Moose on the loose? A guardian elf? This is nuts. Had he imagined Alfred? Was all the stress putting him into some weird state of elf hypnosis? Pete's aching body made him pretty sure of Alfred's existence. If this was all real, Alfred was probably right. He should deal with some of the festering issues within his organization. At the mere thought of that, he decided he needed a drink.

Just as he rose to leave the table, his chest tightened, as if a huge elastic band was squeezing it. Spots began flashing in front of his eyes. Then the room went black. Pete crashed to the floor, dragging his place setting down with him. The plate and glasses exploded into tiny splinters. Michelle raced into the kitchen. After a quick look at Pete sprawled on the floor, she dialed 911.

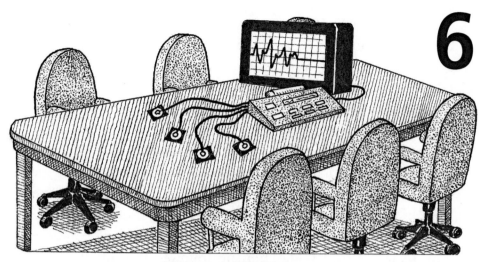

Heart Failure

Pete listened to the steady beeps of the machine monitoring his heartbeat as he lay in his hospital bed. He didn't remember much about the ambulance ride. The following hours were a blur of poking, prodding, questioning, and testing. It wasn't exactly the evening he had planned.

For the first time in what seemed like forever, he was alone. Just him and the rhythmic beeps of the heart monitor. Dr. Yantzi was gone, and Michelle was getting something to eat and making a few phone calls to update their family on his condition.

Pete didn't understand why she was so upset. A panic attack isn't a heart attack, he thought. And he was being monitored overnight just to be sure. Dr. Yantzi didn't waste any time when it became clear that his heart was okay. He started again with his concern for Pete's health – both physical and emotional – along with lifestyle choices that were only making matters worse. When Pete told him that he hadn't filled his prescription for the antidepressants, Dr. Yantzi just shook his head.

"So, cowardly lion, can we crank this thing up to give you a blast of courage? It says here it was made in Kansas."

Pete groaned. His stressed-out imagination seemed to be kicking into overdrive again. Alfred was looking at the heart monitor the way kids look at puppies.

"*Don't touch anything*," Pete shouted. But not a real shout. The world might not see Pete's elf illusion, but it would surely hear the madman screaming in the cardiac unit. "I was afraid you might be back. How do I get rid of you?" The beeps of the heart monitor were escalating sporadically.

"By living up to your name and dealing with your moose problem," Alfred said. Then he followed one of the wires from the machine to the electrode on Pete's chest and pulled hard on it. The sticky tab tore away along with a clump of Pete's chest hair.

"OOOUUCH! I said *don't touch anything, you idiot!*"

The beeping noise went from a trot to a gallop as an alarm sounded. A nurse burst into the room. "Are you all right, Mr. Leonard?"

"Sorry. I was moving around and I guess I pulled this wire off."

The nurse unpeeled the backing of a new tab and then reattached the electrode. The large feathers on Alfred's hat waved as watched the scene.

"I think you'd better take another sedative," the nurse said, producing a pill. "I'll refill your water."

As she turned her back, Alfred picked up the pill and threw it in a perfect arc across the room, through the small bathroom door. It landed in the water of the toilet with a muted plop. "Three points," he declared with a wink and bob of his hat.

After the nurse left the room, Alfred settled into lecture mode. "Do you know that the word 'courage' is a Middle

English word derived from an Old French word for 'heart'? So maybe this is really your courage-monitoring machine."

"This is not a good time for you to be giving me lessons in etymology."

"Aristotle taught that courage is the foundation of all human virtues because it makes the others possible. It starts with facing the fact that you are free to choose your life. You have the free will to define who you are. You aren't stuck with what your circumstances, society, or genes made you. You become what you choose to be. You're a product of your own will. You have chosen to be where you are in life."

"Where is your mute button? How do I shut you off?"

"If Aristotle were here now, he would tell you that you've willed me into your life because you know there are issues you need to deal with."

"For god's sake, don't make him appear too!"

"The strange thing is that freedom isn't easy. It requires individuals to take responsibility for their actions. But most weaklings like you want to escape from freedom. Cowards like you find it too hard to accept responsibility for the life your choices have created. It's much easier – and certainly more popular – to blame fate, luck, or others for where you are. So you chickens create elaborate defense and avoidance mechanisms to hide from the tough issues and avoid making changes to your thinking and lifestyle. You have tranquilized and numbed yourself into just getting by. But Pete, that's just existing. It's not really living. You're a prisoner in a jail you built."

Alfred punctuated his point by jabbing Pete hard in the side with his bony finger. The beeping started its upward tick again.

"I've been thinking about the moose," Pete said with a note of resignation. "And I realize I do need to deal with a few things on my team."

Alfred slapped Pete on the shoulder. "Now you're talking sense! True courage isn't to be fearless. Courage is facing our fears and dealing with them. We need to find and hunt down our moose!"

"I have been thinking that once I get back to work I need to do some moose hunting."

"Bravo! As Edward said in Shakespeare's *King Henry the Sixth*: 'Strike up the drum; cry Courage! and away.'"

"Great. Now get lost!"

The beeping began to gallop again.

"Good morning, Pete. When did you start wearing glasses?"

"They're new," Pete said. "Until I started wearing them I didn't realize how much I was missing,"

Zoë had worked on the operations management team for about a year now. She headed up the southwestern region and was equally respected for her strong engineering background and technical depth, as well as the lively and creative touch she brought to all her projects. Her effectiveness belied the stereotype of a good-looking blonde without brains and leadership abilities.

After his attack, Pete had a few days at home to think about his job and the other things in his life that had put him in the hospital. Michelle was a wreck, and he didn't want to do that to her again anytime soon. So lying on the couch, he decided that it was time to tackle some of the moose issues in his team. On his drive into the office this morning, his regular radio station had played a Waylon Jennings song. Pete couldn't get one of the lines out of his head:

> *If you have the courage*
> *And you have the heart*
> *That hero just might be you.*

Pete hadn't seen Alfred since the hospital. But his special glasses did make the moose wandering through the office all too visible. He counted about a dozen moose in the herd. Besides the two large bulls, there were three cows, a few cute baby calves with long spindly legs, and a couple of mid-sized ones that might have been adolescents. Pete shuddered at the thought of hormonal teenage moose charging around the office. He wore his glasses occasionally and carefully. When he had them on, he could brush up against the moose and feel their rough fur. And he could feel and smell the hot and swampy breath of the big bull moose that seemed to follow him everywhere. But he made sure not to make eye contact with them; the few times that he had, they had lowered their racks and prepared to charge.

Pete had called a meeting of his department's management team. As Duncan came into the room, Pete noticed that a teenage moose trailed behind him and jumped up on the table beside the big bull that was already there. Pete quickly took his glasses off when the teenager turned defiantly toward him and lowered its head while pawing the table with an oversized front hoof.

Duncan was in charge of the central region – their largest and busiest area. He was in his early fifties and had joined NMTS from a competitor about five years ago. He could be gruff and was easily ruffled. His mostly gray and neatly trimmed beard didn't seem to match his light brown hair. He settled his large frame into a chair with a sigh.

The rest of Pete's team shuffled in and assumed their regular spots around the table for their weekly meeting. Pete glanced at the clock. Another late start, he thought. Half of the team members had their heads down and were busily typing and thumbing e-mail and text responses.

"Before we start today's meeting, I'd like to introduce an idea I picked up at Jason Reynard's workshop," Pete said. He reached under the table and pulled out two large shopping bags. He withdrew a small stuffed moose for each person and passed them around the table.

"They're cute," Zoë said as she examined hers. Other team members looked puzzled or bemused.

Pete filled them in on the workshop he had attended. "Jason used the metaphor of Moose on the Table to open up conversations about issues that many people in a team know are problems but won't talk about or do anything about."

"Like the ALIGN project," Li said. As the operations coordinator, she managed the department's call center, where customer requests for service or support were assessed, prioritized, and dispatched. Li was short and slight with straight black hair that matched her straight-laced and direct approach.

ALIGN was the corporation's major project to get all departments using a common computer system that integrated key organizational functions, such as customer records, accounting and HR systems, operational and service logistics, and sales forecasting. The project's delays, heavy time demands, and department versus department conflict led to many frustrated people around the company. The project became widely mocked as an acronym for A Ludicrous Investment in Garbage and Nonsense.

"As if the Truth Fairy is suddenly going to show up and tell senior management how ALIGN is pulling this company down," Duncan said, shoving his stuffed moose to one side.

"Although ALIGN is having a very big impact on operations, I don't think there is much point in tackling that one," Pete said. "We're stuck with it. But what are some other moose we might try to hunt down?"

No one spoke.

"Well, let's continue our meeting and see if any other moose issues come up as we go." Pete put on his glasses and saw that one of the baby moose had joined the other two on the table. He quickly removed his glasses when he saw the big bull turn and look at him.

The managers reported on activities in their areas. There was little discussion. As each speaker droned on, some of the managers furtively read e-mails or shuffled through papers. Occasionally an administrative support person would poke their head in the meeting room door, point at a manager, and motion to have them come out into the hallway. Or a cell phone would vibrate on the meeting-room table, causing the owner to pick it up and whisper "hello" while scurrying for the door.

About forty-five minutes into the review, Pete took an urgent call on his phone and ducked out of the room to avoid disrupting the presenter, Richard. When he returned five minutes later, Li and Richard were having an animated exchange. Richard managed the large and sparsely popu-lated northern region. He was normally the jokester but was not his usual cheery self.

Richard was learning over the table and rubbing his tem-ples. "But we've got to have more timely communication before dispatching technicians to service calls that take hours of driving to reach …"

"And your guys would have all the information they needed if they checked …" Li said.

"They aren't checking because half the time what's there isn't what they need or is out of date and …"

"That's because of this ludicrous ALIGN disaster …"

"Well, either get that fixed or stop blaming us …"

The discussion grew more and more heated over the next ten minutes. Duncan jumped in and supported Richard, saying that he was speaking on behalf of all the regional managers. He made a few cynical remarks that were personal jabs at Li's leadership and "the lack of high performance standards on her team." He told her that her team "always focuses on fixing the blame instead of fixing the problem. If they did their jobs, all of us in the regions could get ours done."

Li heaved a big sigh and clamped her lips tight. The three managers had reached a sullen impasse. So Pete said, "Okay, let's hear the last report and then get into plans for the coming week."

That led to much of the same. The tedium was occasionally enlivened by the exchange of comments wrapped in cynical humor.

When the planning session was over, Pete said, "We're running over time. But as you know, the recent organizational survey appears to show that we have some problems in operations. Morale seems to be down and absenteeism is up. I found many of the written comments quite surprising and disturbing. Doug says he's had calls from a few clients about our best techs leaving. He also pointed out that our service levels are slipping – actually, he said they suck. So in light of these problems, my position is being reviewed."

Some of the managers looked at each other briefly, and a few stared out the window at the cool dark clouds blowing through another drab, gray sky.

"I'd like to invest a few extra minutes in doing some moose hunting," Pete said. "What do you think are our biggest moose?"

"Pete, by moose you mean any issue within this team, just in operations, the whole division, or all of NMTS?" Zoë asked.

"I think we should focus mostly within operations."

"Well, ALIGN is a huge moose," Richard said. "But it seems we can't do anything about it."

"The company's financial condition is another one," Jon said. "We can't get the resources we need and it's sure hurting morale."

Jon looked after the eastern region and was the youngest member of the team. He reminded Pete of himself fifteen years ago. It was one of the big reasons Pete had promoted him, even though others felt he was a little green for the job. Jon could be impatient and impulsive, but he was very hard working – to the detriment of his young family – and devoted to NMTS and operations.

"Not much we can do about that one either," Li said with a sigh.

"How about the organizational survey?" Duncan asked. "It's just opening old wounds and making people even more miserable. There's not much we can do to address a lot of these issues anyway – except get beat up by Doug, HR, and the rest of the upper gods. It must be great to sit on the throne every day and rule by decree."

Then he imitated Doug: " 'Why don't we tell them to fly to work in jetpacks?' But who is it who has to design the jetpacks? Running this survey is a great example. It's all just a bunch of whining and complaining from techs and support staff. And it's really just their perception. It's not reality."

Pete lost track of who was saying what as the floodgates opened and a tsunami of complaints surged through the room.

"How about decision making? We have to wait forever these days to get some of the simplest things approved. Just yesterday I ..."

"Bad attitudes among many staff is a moose. And it's contagious as ..."

"Time management is a huge problem ..."

"That's because of the impossible workload everyone is carrying. And that everything is urgent. We need to set priorities and stick to them. It's crazy trying to do it all ..."

"Nobody listens to anyone else ..."

"And what about e-mail? How many e-mails get sent to folks ten feet away? It's like we sit down with our coffees when we come in and our legs stop working for the rest of the day. Lots of misunderstandings and resentment comes from the ..."

Then Li and Richard got into it again.

"That's very true," Li said. "The survey shows that trust and communications are big problems in operations. And I think a lot of that can be directly traced back to this group. We need to trust and respect each other more so ..."

"There's the pot calling the kettle black," Richard said.

Pete put on his glasses and saw another two moose saunter in and stand along the wall. Zoë excused herself. She was late for a meeting. All it takes is one lead sheep, Pete thought, as Jon and Duncan followed suit, shuffling papers and closing their laptops.

"Okay, okay, I guess we've found a few of the moose lurking in the halls," Pete said. He forgot that nobody else actually saw moose anywhere. "I'd like you all to put the little stuffed moose I gave you on your desk. It's supposed to foster better communications. When people on your team ask about the moose, explain the concept and ask them if they have any moose issues they'd like to discuss. See you all again next week."

On the way back to his office, Pete stopped at the copier. He had an article by Jason Reynard explaining the moose metaphor that he wanted to copy and post on the bulletin board. Duncan's cubicle was across from the copy machine. He and Richard were chatting.

"Well *that* was complete waste of time and oxygen," Duncan said.

"No kidding. And what was with that group gripe tacked on at the end? This company has real problems and handing out cutesy little moose isn't going to solve them! Not counting Doug, the biggest moose in the division was sitting in the chair at the head of the table."

Duncan laughed. "You've got that right. The way Pete runs these meetings has taken us to new lows of irrelevance. We can have meetings or we can do work. We can't do both. It's like we're meeting for the sake of meeting."

"I don't think he's ever made a real decision. He tries to lure us into the famous 'guess what I am thinking' game that leads to some artificial consensus or he waffles on the smallest issues ..."

"Especially decisions that – god forbid – might conflict with what Doug may or may not be thinking. Or anything that deals with anything that might be important."

Pete was stunned. He had no idea that Duncan and Richard thought so poorly of him. He quickly finished making his copy and scurried back to his office. His chest was feeling tight again. He washed down two pills with a swig of coffee. Scrolling through his crowded inbox, he came across a message announcing Damali's resignation. He wasn't surprised, given the POETS Society meeting at Rocky and Bullwinkle's. What a major loss she will be for this division, he thought.

Pete was hit by a cool blast of air as he headed out the front door toward his car. The evening sky threatened still more rain in what was becoming one of the wettest springs on record.

"Did you have a nice day in the corporate jungle, Mr. Faint-hearted Lion? Or did you see a few shadows that sent you cowering back to your den?"

"Oh joy! You're just what I need right now!" Pete said. "I was just thinking about how the sudden appearance of my least favorite hallucination would be a delightful way to cap off another banner day at NMTS."

As they walked, Alfred's hat feathers bobbed up and down in time with his longbow, which was strung over one shoulder. "You created this disastrous day for yourself with the unbelievably clumsy way you tried to deal with the moose issues," he said. "Did you realize that you actually increased the size of the herd today?"

"That's what I get for following the advice of my insightful guardian elf."

Alfred took his longbow off his shoulder, pulled an arrow out of his quiver, and then took one of Pete's stuffed moose, threw it high in the air, and reduced it to fluff and cloth with his deadly aim.

"Hey, those things aren't free, you know."

"But they're incredibly expensive if you don't use them right. We've got to get you some help before that herd in your office crowds out more people like Damali."

"I don't need any more help from you. Just leave me alone." Pete turned and walked quickly down the steps toward the parking lot.

"I think I know who can help us," Alfred said, running in front of Pete. He stopped suddenly and Pete tripped over his longbow. Crashing down the last step, he felt his left ankle twist under him. The pain shot up his leg as he fell to the sidewalk below.

The Mighty Maynard

Cy Garnet rushed over to Pete. "Are you okay, Pete? That was a nasty fall." He helped Pete hobble over to the stairs.

Cy was Doug's boss. He was sixty-one, with a full head of thick and wavy silver hair. His clean-shaven face provided a perfect frame for his broad and easy grin. He was well-liked and respected around the office, in no small part due to his outgoing and friendly personality.

It was Cy who had initially recruited Pete to join the company and was his boss in the early go-go years. Pete considered him the best coach and mentor he'd ever had. As the company grew, their careers moved in different directions. Soon Pete was no longer reporting directly to Cy, but they did stay in touch over the years. "The last of the trailblazers," Cy always joked when introducing Pete to colleagues. Doug was jealous of their bond and did all he could to block any contact between them.

Pete picked at the small pebbles embedded in his scraped palms. "Thanks," he said sheepishly. "My ankle is really sore.

I must've twisted it pretty hard." He rubbed the puffy area around his ankle. Steadying himself on the handrail, he stood and slowly put weight on his left foot. He winced as intense pain shot up his leg. "Not exactly my most elegant moment. Can you give me a hand over to my car?"

"Maybe I should take you to the hospital."

"Thanks, but I'll be all right once I get home and put my foot up. Luckily it's my left leg. I only need it for walking." Pete forced another smile, but it didn't make it past a grimace. "I don't need it to drive."

When Pete was finally in and buckled up, Cy asked, "How's the moose hunting going in operations, Pete?"

"How did you know about that?" Maybe he wasn't going crazy, Pete thought. Could somebody else also see the moose?

"I saw some of your team carrying stuffed moose around the office today. I've been to a Reynard workshop or two. I liked the Moose-on-the-Table concept. Have you named any moose yet?"

"Well, we have a list of concerns, but that's about all we had time for. We haven't really done anything with them."

"So you'll need to prioritize the biggest ones and get your team busy dealing with them."

Cy was never one to beat around the bush, but he was supportive in helping you solve your problems. Pete preferred this approach to Doug's "leadership" edicts.

"I guess so," Pete said. "But most of the issues are out of our hands. And with so much else going on, I don't really know if we have the time to spend on this type of exercise. At this point I'm just hoping we've opened up some communications."

"If ever there was a time for operations to shine, this is it," Cy said. The company is really up against a wall. Time isn't on our side. Your group has a big role to play in turning this thing around and getting us out of this mess." Cy paused for a second before continuing. "I have to say that I was really surprised by your organizational survey results. It looks like you've got some big moose to deal with. Is there anything corporate can do to help?"

"I was thinking that I might sit down with Heather and get her ideas on how to turn things around."

"I'd strongly encourage you to do that. You and I go back a long way. You know I've always believed in and supported you. I know you've had some setbacks in the past few years. I just hope you haven't been knocked down too far by all that. I'm concerned about you. Just let me know if I can help in any way."

Pete smiled through his pain. "Thanks, Cy. I'm sure we'll get along."

Pete parked his car in the garage. If it wasn't so painful, the hop to the house would have been comical. Shifting from the wall to the handrail to the top of the garbage bin, he cursed a blue streak all the way to the door. Michelle wasn't home, but at least Amanda was there to help him to his easy chair in front of the television.

Amanda loved her dad and he knew it. But she'd reached those teenage years where he was no longer her idol. And his latest injury only contributed to her growing conviction that Dad was a fat klutz as well as one of the dumbest and most out-of-touch men that ever drew a breath. She dutifully popped some leftovers in the microwave and put a bag of ice cubes on his ankle before heading to the mall to meet her friends. Staying at home with her invalid father wasn't an option.

Pete munched away on his half-warmed potatoes and chicken. With all the advances in the modern world, he thought, why couldn't someone develop a microwave capable of heating a full plate of food evenly? Just as his mind began to drift into equally inane and relaxing thoughts, it quickly corrected itself and he was back thinking about work. It had been this way for weeks. It was like he was on auto-pilot. No matter what he did to change the course, he always ended up on the same stretch of road.

The whole moose thing and all the poking and prodding from Alfred were very disturbing. It made no sense. If Alfred was an hallucination, he was a very realistic one, Pete thought, rubbing the shoulder the elf punched a few days earlier. Was all the anxiety and stress finally sending him over the edge? One thing was certain: he wasn't imagining his throbbing ankle.

Pete took a deep drink from his wine glass. He reached for the bottle of stress beans on the table. It was sitting on top of Jason Reynard's leadership book. Where had that come from? He distinctly remembered leaving the book at the workshop because he'd had no intention of ever reading it. He picked it up and flipped through the pages and popped the cap off the pill bottle.

Pete found himself not exactly reading but skimming the contents. But what he saw he had to admit was pretty good. Furthermore, it was relevant to his situation. That's odd, he thought, someone had highlighted a few of the passages in the chapter on fear. Pete noticed the cap was still off the pain relievers. He hadn't taken any pills, and his headache was gone. He put the cap back on the bottle.

He started to read some of the highlighted parts.

Regrets for actions we don't take drips acid on our soul.

That seems harsh, he thought, but he understood the point. The conversation he had overheard between Duncan and Richard was a big splash of acid. And not because of their critical opinions. He knew they fed off each other's negativity. No, what hurt most was how right they were. His meetings weren't very effective, and he hadn't handled the moose-hunting exercise well at all. Worst of all, he knew that his judgment and decision making had really slipped.

But when they accused him of not taking on Doug – that wasn't fair. What good would he be to anyone if he got passed over or canned for making a CLM – a career-limiting move – or even a CEM – a career-ending move? It's better to go along to get along, he thought. All he had to do was get through this rough patch to keep his job and hang on "to the lifestyle to which he'd become accustomed," as his alimony settlement with Chantal so eloquently put it.

Fear is all in our head. It's a mind game we play on ourselves. For example, a well-produced and realistic horror movie can make our skin crawl and pulse race, and can strike terror deep into our hearts. Extreme stress and physical changes can be clearly recorded in our bodies. Yet the movie is just bits of sound and light images projected on a screen. It's not really happening.

Pete thought about how whenever Amanda went to a horror movie, she had to sleep on the carpet beside Pete and Michelle's bed because she was so terrified. Pete had a feeling it wasn't something she shared with her friends. He'd keep telling her there was nothing to worry about – that it was all in her head. But her imagination ran wild when she lay in her own bed, turning routine night-time household sounds into a soundtrack for murder and mayhem. Fear certainly produces a powerful and irrational emotional response in her, he thought, chuckling.

Fear is a powerful form of imagery – it's our own terrifying optical illusion.

The next sentence had a big arrow pointing at it from the margin.

What would you do if you weren't afraid?

Pete's mind took a second to process the question. If I weren't afraid … I'd deal with Doug and get rid of some big moose. I'd find a better way to identify the major moose in our team and pull everyone together to address the ones we can work with. I'd stop going along with things I don't agree with. I'd learn how to give better presentations and run better meetings …

"And face your problems like a lion – without cowardly booze and pills."

Pete dropped the book, startled by Alfred's voice and appearance beside his chair.

Alfred picked up the glass of wine and poured it over Pete's head. Pete cursed and jumped to his feet as the wine ran down the front of his shirt. It was just after his body had sprung up that he remembered his ankle. It felt like hours for his left foot to hit the floor in what he knew was going to be excruciating and unavoidable pain. He yelped and released the muscles in his leg to take the weight off of it as he toppled helplessly onto the carpet. Breaking his fall with his left arm, he thought he heard a crack. The string of profanities streaming from his mouth would have shocked a sailor.

"There's the effect of some more fear for you," Alfred said merrily as he looked down at Pete lying on the carpet rubbing and flexing his left wrist. Pete's expletive-laced torrent continued unabated. For Alfred it only added to the hilarity. "Since I don't understand all the new words ye moderns have added to the olde English language, I'll take most of those as compliments and pretend not to have heard the others."

Then Alfred smiled and grandly reintroduced himself: "Alfred, your guardian elf, at your service, Mr. Leonard." He removed his feathered hat and swept it down across his body as he bent into a low bow.

"I don't *^#@*&! believe this!" Pete's face was beet red as he struggled to stand without using either his left arm or left leg.

"In case you were unsure, I did understand that very bad word," said Alfred. "I think you need to control your language a bit, so we can keep this suitable for family viewing." He helped Pete back into his chair. Then he went into the bathroom and brought back a towel for Pete to soak up some of the wine he was wearing.

Pete maintained a glum silence as he dried himself. He finished by putting the ice pack on his left wrist. He glowered as he watched the elf pick up the management book from the floor.

"You haven't yet read the passage on fear that most applies to you," Alfred said as he flipped through the book. "Here it is." He proceeded to read it to Pete.

Fear lets the air out of the tires that roll us along through life. If enough air is released, the tires will be damaged and we'll be forced to slow down or stop to address the problem.

"Your tires are flat, big guy, and this spare won't do you any good." He poked Pete's ample belly with the book. Pete whacked the book away. It flew across the room, knocking three small porcelain figures off a side table. Two of them broke into tiny pieces.

Alfred put down his longbow and sat on the chair to Pete's right. "Watching your pathetic attempt at moose hunting with your team this afternoon reminded me of an old hunter legend. Years ago there was a mighty hunter named Maynard.

His name meant 'brave strength,' from the Germanic elements 'magin' – 'strength' and 'hard' – 'brave, hardy.'

"Maynard's elk instincts, hunting skills, and marksmanship with a longbow were legendary. He could pretty much find and kill elk at will. His hunting success was many times that of any other hunter. So his party of followers increased and he became the head of a large and very well-fed band of hunters that roamed through olde England's great forests, meadows, and glens.

"As the years passed, Mighty Maynard spent more and more time lounging in the sun and basking in his own glory. He loved nothing more than the praise of others for his unmatched prowess and legendary feats. He began wearing a set of elaborately decorated elk horns and spent evenings sitting by the fire on a very large and intricately carved oak chair as elk roasted for the evening feast. As time passed, his temper became more volatile. He carried a large and gnarly walking stick to club hunters who dared make a mistake during a hunt or were just unlucky enough to be in the way when Mighty Maynard was in a foul mood. Everyone knew of his temper. They were also well aware that he'd killed a few hunters and broken bones in many others. No one talked about that.

"Maynard's second in command was Alvin, which means 'elf friend,' from the Old English name Ælfwine, which was formed of the elements 'ælf' – elf – and 'wine' – 'friend.'"

"Your obsession with the meaning of names is getting really irritating," Pete said.

"Words create our worlds, my friend. There's a deeper meaning to words and the world around you that you're choosing to ignore. That's a big reason you've got so many elk, or I should say moose, in your life."

Pete rested his head on his right hand and stared at the floor.

"Meanwhile, back to our story," Alfred said. "Unlike you, Alvin was a master storyteller. He earned his powerful position because of his ability to dramatize Mighty Maynard's greatest hunting feats. Maynard never tired of Alvin's evening entertainment. The rest of the hunters learned to look enthusiastic and cheer in all the right places during Alvin's repeated re-enactments. The Mighty Maynard had encouraged this participation after he walked over and whacked a few bored-looking hunters with his big stick when Alvin first started telling his tales.

"Eventually Mighty Maynard's elk horns, huge wooden chair, and Alvin's growing number of props meant that moving around to track the elk was becoming increasingly difficult. So when the hunting party found a spot on the edge of a forest with both a river and a large cave in the nearby hills, Mighty Maynard set up a permanent camp. He and his hunters roamed further and further to find elk to feed their growing settlement. Maynard stayed behind more often. He was growing larger and was finding the long hunts tiring. Alvin assured him that participating was beneath a Mighty Hunter of his standing anyway.

"One evening, before eating their dismal rations, three of the best hunters came to Alvin just out of earshot of Mighty Maynard. The elk feasts of old had been reduced to a few occasional bits of meat mixed with roots, berries, and whatever else the hunters could find on their long walks home. They often shot only one or no elk at all.

"'We are barely finding elk any more,' one of them whispered.

"'We need to pack up camp and move further inland to find a herd,' another hunter added.

"'There's growing talk among the hunters about forming their own band or joining another one,' the third hunter said.

"'What are you whispering about over there?' Mighty Maynard bellowed, pointing his stick at Alvin. The other hunters trembled and slunk back toward some behind them.

"'Uh, well, sir … we were, we were, uh, just comparing notes on a big herd that may be in the area. Tomorrow's hunt promises to be bountiful.'

"'That's good. Glad to hear it. I would hate to have to move camp from this very comfortable spot.' Mighty Maynard settled back in his chair, took another deep drink of his tankard of mead, and sleepily closed his eyes. 'Tell us the story of the day I brought down this big buck,' he said, pointing to the enormous set of antlers he was wearing.

"The next day the hunters returned home with no elk. They did see signs that another hunting party had shot and butchered two large ones. But they brought back only roots and berries for their meager evening meal. When Maynard asked Alvin about this, Alvin told him that many in their band heard a vegetarian diet was healthier than all that high-cholesterol red meat anyway."

Alfred snickered and waited for Pete to respond. With his head still resting on his right hand, Pete moved only his eyes toward Alfred and said, "Very funny," in a dry monotone.

"Just wanting to see if you're still with me, big guy."

Alfred knocked Pete's arm that was propping up his head. Pete's body slumped sharply to the right. He didn't say a word as he gave Alfred a stony stare and settled himself into the back of his chair.

"Alvin tried his best to sound casual in telling Mighty Maynard that another band of hunters was in the area. Maynard's eyes opened wide as he grasped for his big stick. 'But not to worry, sir,' Alvin said. 'They are probably rabbit or deer eaters.'

"'All right. No point in our getting excited about that, then, is there?' Maynard replied, as he closed his eyes and his stick fell to the side. Alvin needed to tell Maynard that a group of their best hunters and families had left the band. But this wasn't the right time.

"Over the following weeks a depressing pattern emerged as more hunters left and those remaining returned with nothing to share. As he drank more mead to kill the hunger pains and keep his spirits up, Mighty Maynard asked Alvin where his best hunters and their families had gone.

"'Oh that. It's nothing, sir. Their skills were really slipping and they've lost their hunting instincts. I encouraged them to join bands that eat easier game.'

"'Good thinking,' Mighty Maynard replied. 'We're big game hunters and we don't want our standards to slip because a few people can't cut it anymore.'

"'My thoughts exactly, sir!'

"It wasn't too long before there were no elk because all the hunters had left. 'What's going on, Alvin?' Mighty Maynard asked. 'Where is everyone?'

"Alvin made sure he was well outside the range of the big stick. 'They've all left us, sir,' he said.

"'Left us?' Mighty Maynard started to bellow and rose from his great carved chair. 'How could that happen after all that I did for them?' He sank back into his throne.

"Alvin shrugged his shoulders.

"'I can't understand it,' Mighty Maynard said. 'Everything was going so well.'"

Alfred leaned back in his chair and looked at Pete. "Does any of that sound familiar?"

"It sounds like more of your crap about hunting moose. If I wasn't hurting so much, I'd drop-kick you right back where you belong, along with all your ancient campfire stories ..."

"Who are you going to drop-kick, honey? Who are you talking to?"

Pete turned to see Michelle standing in the doorway in her wet coat with packages in her hands.

"Oh, hi. I didn't hear you come in. How was your day?"

"Mine was fine. But what's going on with you and this destruction?" Michelle looked at the shattered figurines, the book lying open in the middle of the family-room floor, Pete's wet shirt, a good bathroom guest towel over a chair arm, a dirty dish on a side table, an ice pack on Pete's left wrist, and what looked to be a wounded ankle resting on a foot stool.

"Oh yeah. I tripped and sprained my ankle on the way home tonight. When I got home, Amanda warmed up some leftovers for me. Sorry about the mess. I was stumbling around a bit and knocked a few things over. I'll clean up." Pete tried to get out of his chair.

"And then I come in and find you babbling to yourself about drop-kicking someone? Pete, we really need to talk. I've been thinking long and hard about you and about us. I don't know how much longer I can continue to sit by and watch you self-destruct. You really need professional help. In fact, I think that we really need help as a couple."

Pete could feel the blood rushing to his face. How could Michelle be so insensitive to what he was going through? The ensuing argument was one for the highlight reels. Pete was a dirty fighter. He never failed to raise anything, no matter how small, that would help him score points. He knew that winning this type of fight wasn't important, but he couldn't help himself once the battle begun.

Fifteen minutes later and with tears streaming down her cheeks, Michelle dug out her car keys and headed for the front door. "If you're not willing to see a therapist or counselor with me, I am not sure we can make it together. I need time to think. I won't be home tonight." She softly closed the door behind her.

Pete was alone. Again.

Moose Tracks

Three days after spraining his ankle and wrist, Pete was still moving stiffly. If he didn't feel like an old man before, he was definitely feeling it now. And to make matters worse, the moose population in the office had multiplied. They were growing more restless as they fought for turf.

Pete decided to do something about it. He dialed Heather's number.

"Hi, Heather. This is Pete Leonard. I'd like to get together and talk about how I could do some moose-hunting exercises with my team. Please get back to me with a time for us to meet."

Pete knew that Heather was terrible at keeping her online calendar up to date, so booking a meeting without speaking to her directly would have been pointless.

When the familiar beep of Pete's phone began, he was at the photocopier. He hobbled back to his office as quickly as he could, providing a cheap laugh for anyone watching.

It was Heather, and she took a few seconds to think about her schedule. "How about 10:30 this morning?"

"That sounds great. I'll bring the coffee. What do you take?"

Pete arrived at the meeting with two coffees in hand. On the conference table were a couple of Rocky and Bullwinkle coasters. "I'm not sure where those came from," Pete said, as he put the coffees down. As he gently lowered himself into his chair, he thought he saw Bullwinkle throw a wink at him. Heather didn't see Pete raise his eyebrows and sigh.

"Are you all right, Pete?" Heather asked. "You look like you've been in a wreck."

"A wreck would be easier to explain, believe me," Pete said. "Thanks for meeting with me this morning. Since you coordinated the organizational survey and are familiar with Jason Reynard's Moose-on-the-Table concept, I thought I might pick your brain about how I can deal with some moose that are taking over my department."

"I'm happy to help. Where would you like to start?"

Pete told her about his failed moose-hunting exercise a few days earlier. "I've been ignoring issues or putting them off for a long time and they aren't going anywhere. In fact they seem to be multiplying. I have to tell you, I wasn't even paying that much attention in Jason's workshop. But the more I think about it, the more I realize that we really need to deal with these problems before they get any bigger. But they're already so big I don't know where to start."

"Well, the key thing is that you want to start. These are usually difficult conversations to have, for you, and for your team. There are issues we're all afraid of addressing. But if we don't, then we can't see what's really going on. As the leader, sometimes it takes more courage to sit down and listen than it does to stand up and speak."

Pete nodded and sipped his coffee.

"Pete, you already know what conclusions I drew from reviewing your organization's survey responses. I could add more of my thoughts and observations from talks I've had and work I've done with the members of your team. But I think you could really benefit from a fresh, outside perspective and a well-tested process. You're too close to the situation to deal with it objectively. I recommend we bring Jason in to facilitate a moose-hunting expedition."

"That sounds like a good idea, but Doug would never approve it."

"I know how concerned Cy is about what's happening here. I think he could twist Doug's arm a bit."

"Given Doug's history with any sort of 'soft' stuff, Cy might have to break it."

Pete and Heather went on to review the organizational survey findings and discuss the dynamics of Pete's management team. As they were wrapping up, Pete said, "I'm not sure how useful Jason's help will be. But I'll meet with him and see what he can add – if I can get approval from Doug."

"Let me see what I can do," Heather said.

The next afternoon Pete received an e-mail from Doug. The subject line – "Outside Consultant" – didn't look promising. The message read: "We're drowning in red ink and you need to have all your attention focused on fixing the problems in your shop. I understand you want to hire a consultant to do your job for you. This is a waste of time and money, but Heather has convinced Cy that I should find money in the budget to cover your leadership abdication. So give me a proposal on what you want to do. It had better be good."

It's great when you have the enthusiastic support of your boss, Pete thought. He replied that he didn't know if he wanted to use Jason Reynard, but he'd meet with him, get back to Doug with a proposal if necessary.

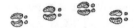

It was yet another rainy morning and the drive into work was complicated by an overturned beer truck, which closed two lanes on the expressway. There was a contradiction in terms if there ever was one, Pete thought, as he idled along in bumper-to-bumper traffic. He was meeting Jason and Heather at 9:00. At this pace, the meeting would likely be another late start.

But everyone managed to make it on time. Pete sat down at his desk at 8:55 with his first big mug of coffee. He washed down a few pills to reduce the throbbing that was starting at the back of his neck. Heather and Jason joined him at the small table in his cramped office.

Heather was anxious to get started. "As we agreed, I gave Jason a copy of the organizational survey and briefed him on our big financial crunch," she told Pete. "I'll leave the specifics of your own organizational and management team issues to you."

"What would you like to get out of a moose-hunting exercise?" Jason asked Pete.

"One of my objectives is to get at the root of the trust and communication problem you saw in our survey. I'd also like to get our management team working together more effectively and reduce some of the conflict. As well, we need to set some priorities and plans around improving our service/quality levels and improving our financial performance. But I'd especially like to figure out what our biggest moose are and how to get rid of them. I suppose all these things are interconnected somehow."

"They usually are," Jason said, with a reassuring smile. "If dealing with these issues was easy or straightforward, you wouldn't need me."

Pete was getting a good feeling for the first time in a long while.

Jason went on to explain that the most successful process involved a combination of one-on-one interviews, observing a few management meetings, an open-ended e-mail survey of the management team, and focus-group discussions with small groups of front-line staff representing a cross-section of the operations department.

"Of course, all this is very confidential," Jason said. "I'll prepare a summary for you and your management team, focusing on the key themes that have emerged. We'll use that as the basis of our two-day offsite management retreat and ..."

"There's no way I can take my whole management team away for two days at this point," Pete said. "We're too busy for that. Can't you just give me your report and recommendations and we'll take it from there?"

"I'm not here as an expert to tell you what to do. I do have leadership expertise and I'm rarely without an opinion. But my role is to help you name the moose and facilitate discussion on how you and your management team are going to deal with them. I'll then guide you in setting your plans to move you forward. A report on its own wouldn't do that for you."

"But do we really need to take a few days away from the business?"

"The reason many management teams get themselves into trouble is because they are so busy working *in* the business or team. You need to learn to balance that with working *on* the business or team. You've probably heard the definition of insanity as 'continuing to use the same approach but expecting different outcomes ...'"

Heather jumped in to lend Jason some support. "When would you get the time to work on these issues if you didn't get away from them for a more objective look at things?"

"I can see the value in taking this approach," Pete said. "I'm just not sure we have the time to do this. Can we wait until I review your report and then decide?"

"There's a big problem with doing that. As everyone gives me their perspectives on your group's issues and improvement opportunities, they need to know their input is going to be seriously considered and addressed. I need to be able to explain exactly how that is going to happen in order to give participants reason to believe it's worth their time to participate."

When Pete said nothing, Jason continued, "I reviewed your survey, and from what Heather tells me, I suspect the 'snicker factor' is very high around here. Like many organizations, people in your group probably have high levels of survey fatigue. They've been surveyed to death. Worse, they probably never saw any results or actions."

Too true, Pete thought. He could see the value in the full approach Jason was outlining. But he could also hear Doug bellowing his profane reaction out his corner office suite.

"I'd like to ask you a related, but very critical question, Pete," Jason said. "Are you prepared to deal with all the moose issues raised by this process or are there areas that you consider off-limits? The worst thing you can do is have me out raising expectations that some of these long-standing or growing issues will be addressed and then not deal with them. That actually leaves you in a worse position than if you had never asked the questions in the first place. All you'll do is reinforce the cynics who say, 'I told you nothing would happen.' If you think you have a moose problem now, try that approach!"

"You didn't happen to see the moose on your way through the office when you came in this morning, did you?" Pete asked.

"I can guess what some of the moose are from my preparations, but our assumptions can often get in the way of learning what's really going on. That's why they aren't being dealt with effectively since …"

"No, I mean did you see moose out there in our office?"

Jason looked at Pete before turning to Heather. "Moose on the Table is a metaphor for issues that aren't being addressed," he said.

Heather looked at Pete with concern. "Harold mentioned that you said you were terrified of a moose on the road the night he took you home from Rocky and Bullwinkle's. You're not literally seeing moose, are you?"

"Don't be silly," Pete said with a nervous titter. "Lately I've been a lot of things, but delusional isn't one of them. I, uh … I know this is just a metaphor."

Pete shifted in his chair to buy himself a little time. A huge brown shadow drifted past his left shoulder. He looked at Jason. "To answer your question, the only moose I am less prepared to deal with are the ones out of our control."

"Are you open to exploring all the moose and debating which ones you can eliminate, influence, or learn to live with? It does take real courage for you as a leader to see yourself and your behavior through the eyes of others. I call them courageous conversations."

"I can't say I am looking forward to some of these discussions. But we do need to get rid of a bunch of moose in this office." He could have sworn he heard a snort and the sound of a big hoof pawing the carpet behind him.

"Good. I'm glad to hear that. Successful moose hunting comes from the willingness within the group – and especially from its leader – to address painful issues. It also involves the right timing, skilled facilitation, and an effective process – especially one that is safe for everyone involved. I hope this doesn't sound immodest, but I will be bringing years of experience facilitating these types of exercises and a strong process to the table. Your group sounds like it's ready to have courageous conversations. If you're truly open to hearing what you probably don't want to hear and ready to talk about things you've been avoiding, this exercise will move you and your management team forward."

"I think I'm ready," Pete said. "So how does this work?"

The conversation turned to the logistical details of who Jason would talk to, what e-mail survey questions he might ask, and which management meetings he would attend. The meeting concluded with Jason agreeing to send Pete a proposal detailing the process and its costs. As Jason and Heather left his office, Pete put on his moose glasses and counted three large moose pawing the carpet and snorting at Jason. When Pete returned to his desk, he noticed that the rain had finally ended and the clouds were thinning. He saw a ray of sunshine feebly cutting through the sky.

A few days later Jason's proposal arrived by e-mail. It clearly and convincingly outlined the process he would use and the outcomes Pete could expect.

Pete forwarded the proposal to Doug with a note that he'd met with Jason and felt very good about what he was proposing, since it would get at many of the issues on the organizational survey and within his management team. Pete told Doug he had signed the proposal back to Jason and was patching together the fees by pulling funds from a couple of budget categories that were running below projections – especially the training budget – and deferring the filling of a support position that had been approved. It's much easier to ask for forgiveness than permission, he thought as he hit the send button.

Doug's reply was almost immediate. "I am *astounded* that you're proceeding with this process right now. Talk about bad judgment! We need every dollar we can get and you don't have the time to have some consultant taking people away from their real jobs. I want this stopped *immediately*. Cancel the contract and get out there and show some real leadership."

Pete replied with a suggestion that Doug speak to Heather about this, since she was such a strong supporter of going ahead. He never heard back from Doug on the matter. Later he learned that – as expected – Doug had sent an e-mail to Heather about halting the process, Heather had talked to Cy, and Cy had then convinced Doug to let the moose-hunting work proceed.

As impossible as it seemed, Doug's ongoing daily barrage of e-mails to Pete became even more caustic.

Pete and Jason were seated in Pete's cluttered office four weeks after their first meeting. Jason had just completed a series of front-line staff focus groups, personal interviews with each of Pete's management team, and a follow-up e-mail management-team survey. He had also sat in on a few of Pete's weekly management team meetings. Today's meeting with Pete was to review Jason's findings and prepare for the two-day management team retreat scheduled for the end of next week.

"With only a few exceptions, I found people throughout your organization fairly willing to open up and tell me what they really believe are the key issues and improvement opportunities facing the operations department," Jason said.

"There was actually a lot of emotion and pent-up anger in many of the focus-group sessions and one-on-one interviews. That's a positive sign. It shows just how much people in your organization care about this company and that they want to help turn things around. Your organization has clearly not yet advanced to the more deadly stage of apathy. But that will come next if you don't respond to the issues that I've uncovered. Most people here have high energy for change and a strong desire to be part of the solution. But they're extremely frustrated with the lack of focus and a process to make it happen."

Jason reached into his tan leather briefcase and pulled out two copies of his report and handed one of them to Pete. It was a few pages stapled together with Jason's company logo in the top left corner.

"This is what we'll be using at the retreat," Jason said. "I wanted to meet with you today to walk you through it and talk about how we'll approach these discussions with your management team."

He then proceeded to identify the top operations department moose as communications, setting priorities, misaligned processes and systems, decision making, accountability, and leadership.

"Well, that about covers everything," Pete said. "I've totally screwed up. I guess I should resign now."

"These are big challenges. One of the reasons NMTS is in such a bind is because of these complex and interconnected problems. The operations department is both a symptom carrier of the larger company problems and a major contributor to the company's difficulties. But these are all very fixable issues – if, and only if, you and your management team are ready to harness the talent and energy that's evident throughout your group."

Jason went through each of the bullet points listed under each issue, giving a preview of what he planned to discuss with the management team at the retreat. Pete asked questions to clarify points and identified a few areas needing further discussion and clarification with the management team. Pete wasn't surprised by most of what he heard. He could feel a three-pill headache developing as he thought about the discussions that would have to happen.

When they got to the leadership issue, it became clear that front-line staff were talking about the management team. However, the management team was really pointing to Pete's leadership as the key issue to be addressed. Jason asked Pete how he felt about his personal focus, time management, and organization.

Pete popped a couple of pills into his mouth and washed them down with a big swig of extra-strength coffee. Pursing his lips, he replied, "Could be better."

Jason agreed. He quoted a line one of Pete's managers often used to describe Pete's idea of multitasking as "multi-masking." He was referring to Pete's disorganization and lack of focus. Jason added that he'd seen Pete in action, constantly juggling phone calls, e-mails, and meetings with no real sense of priority or overall strategy.

Pete conceded that this could be true.

"Perhaps you let too many people 'should' on you," Jason suggested. "It's so easy to succumb to the 'tyranny of the shoulds.' So others start to drive your agenda and priorities rather than you consciously managing your own time."

That one hurt because it hit the bull's-eye.

Jason traced this problem to the lack of personal coaching and development that most of Pete's management team had isolated as a major challenge. "They have a lot of respect for your experience and expertise. They'd love to help you more and tap into that expertise. But you're either too busy or don't seem interested in providing coaching."

Jason concluded with feedback to Pete on his victimitis. "It looks and sounds to me as if you often bring a defeatist attitude into your meetings and interactions with your managers and even front-line staff when addressing bad news or the latest problem. Since a team is always looking to its leader for how to feel about problems that come along, they follow you right into Pity City."

Pete admitted that he occasionally let his frustration show. "It's been pretty tough to stay positive, given everything we're going through."

"I can understand that. And this is the very time that you need to lead your team above the line and stay in Navigator territory."

Pete was finally beginning to see where he could improve. It was making a lot of sense. He really had slipped into negativity, and his leadership was suffering. He knew what he was capable of. It was becoming painfully obvious to him that he was nowhere close to where he should be performing. He wasn't sure what had happened to cause the decline, but he was sick and tired of living like this.

"I'm really glad you're open to this Pete," Jason said. "I think you're finally ready for change. The best way we can eliminate your moose is if we have courageous conversations at the retreat about these issues, the team's dynamics, and your leadership approaches. Are you ready for that?"

"Yes, I think I am. It won't be easy, but I know it needs to be done."

When Pete returned to his office, he was confronted by a very large and angry bull moose standing on his desk. Papers and books were scattered all over the floor. Good time to go for lunch, Pete thought, and headed for the elevator.

The signs held aloft read: "Stop indecisiveness", "Start clear priorities", "Keep using expertise", "Be open to feedback", "Stop ineffective meetings", "Stand up to Doug", "Start being positive", "St..."

That Slinking Feeling

Pete paddled frantically. His muscles burned as he realized he was losing the struggle to keep his head above the cold water. His ability to breathe was limited as he expended more and more effort spitting out the flood that threatened to wash into his lungs. As he continued to spit and gasp, he remembered the aquatics medal he had won as a child. Second place behind Eugene Meriwether, the fastest kid in the region. But that was a long time ago, and Pete wasn't in any shape to compete anymore. He'd forgotten how to swim. A lifestyle rich in calories was pulling him under.

He was tired. He was sore. This was it. He surrendered to the inevitability of his own sad end and let himself sink below the waterline. But when he was just a few inches below the surface, his foot touched the bottom. It was a sandbar. He summoned the energy to propel himself above the water once again. Gasping for breath, his heart racing, he hopped up on the sandbar and stood up with elation. He'd made it.

As he reached the shore, the white sandy beach darkened to gray industrial carpet and the poplar trees morphed into walls. He wasn't on a beach at all. He was in his office.

His area was usually busy first thing in the morning as folks shuffled between desks and the coffee room to talk about the latest twist on *Navigator-Survivor-Victim,* this year's surprise TV hit. But today it was deathly quiet as everybody avoided eye contact with him.

He felt naked. Naked and wet. He'd felt each many times, standing in the reception area bracing himself to face the day, but never both together. His reached to pull his handkerchief from his pocket. It was then he realized there was no pocket. There was no jacket. There weren't any pants. He was standing in front of his office door dripping wet in a tiny pair of tight white underwear. Instinctively, he covered the front of his underwear with his hands and backed into his office.

The big menacing bull moose waiting for him there looked ready to charge.

Pete rubbed his eyes as he looked at the moose head again. Its eyes weren't blinking or moving. The head wasn't even attached to a body. It was mounted on a cedar slatted wall. The cedar filled the room with a sharp sweet aroma. Pete was lying in bed drenched in sweat. The bright red numbers on the clock to his left read 3:48.

It took him a few seconds to figure out where he was. He was lying in the Elkhorn Lodge. Tomorrow … no, today … was the first day of the two-day team retreat. The lodge was a three-hour drive from the city. This facility had once been a remote and rustic hunting camp. New owners renovated and modernized the lodge into a small conference resort, retaining the rustic lodge décor. Big and small game and fish were stuffed and mounted everywhere.

Pete tossed and turned as he lay awake wondering where the life he loved had gone and whether the next two days would do anything to help him reclaim it. He took another sleeping pill. It made him drowsy, but sleep was not to be. At 5:51 he gave up and dragged himself out of bed for a shower. After dealing with thirteen e-mails – all marked "urgent" – he headed across the courtyard for the morning session. As he walked across the bridge that arched over the small creek into the conference building, he imagined Alfred saying, "Let the adventure begin." Part of him was excited at the thought, but even then he found himself muttering, "Yeah, right," as he stepped into the foyer.

Pete walked to the front of the room for the standard introduction. "I'd like to thank you for taking time from your busy schedules to attend," he started off. Even as the words spilled from his mouth, he realized that they weren't necessary for a mandatory meeting and probably weren't appreciated either.

He pressed on. "Jason has prepared a report and he and I reviewed it last week. I have to confess, I wasn't too surprised by what he had to say."

Pete looked around at the expressionless faces sitting around the room. "I want to tell you all that over the next couple of days, I am committed to discussing and solving the issues we all know are out there, but are so good at avoiding."

He smiled and a few of the faces also showed a potential crinkle around the corners of their mouths. "I'd especially like to get us to work better as a team and increase the levels of trust and communication among ourselves and throughout the operations department. It's a tall order, given what we've all been through, but I hope that with Jason's help we'll get there."

Pete introduced Jason, who was given a smattering of applause. "I attended his one-day workshop, but it wasn't until I read his book and met him a few more times that I really bought into his approach," he said. "That said, I know that if you come at this with an open mind, we'll be able to get a moose-hunting expedition together when we get back to the office."

Blank stares filled the room.

The retreat participants included Zoë, Li, Richard, Jon, and Duncan. Heather was also invited, for her HR experience and her perspectives from the organizational survey.

Jason began by thanking everyone for their frank and open input. Then he summarized the objectives he'd picked up from the management team during his e-mail survey. The survey had allowed him to name the major moose and rank them by size. He then reiterated that his job was to help the team find ways to address these issues themselves. He turned on his projector and an agenda flashed on the screen at the front of the room. Pete saw that it allowed for time to work on the management team's effectiveness, set plans and priorities, and improve trust and communications.

When they had arrived that morning, everyone was given a copy of Jason's book along with a workbook to help guide them through the sessions. The first exercise was halfway through the workbook, where there was a list of key behaviors to increase meeting effectiveness. Jason asked the group to vote on which ones they felt were most important as ground rules for the retreat. After a few minutes of good-natured ribbing and half-hearted debate, the group eventually settled on the following rules of engagement:

1. Sniping, potshots, or put downs are not allowed.

2. Discussions are to focus on the problem, issue, or behavior and avoid personal put downs, judgmental statements, or sweeping generalizations.

3. Everyone is to participate and stay engaged in the conversation.

4. No cutting each other off, finishing someone else's sentences, or engaging in side conversations.

5. Those with dissenting opinions are at least to feel their point of view was heard.

6. Phones, pagers, e-mail devices, and non-participants are not to interrupt the meeting.

On the last point, Jason joked about how some groups have a rule that if a phone or any communication device goes off, the offender had to buy the group a drink at the bar when the session let out.

"Now that's a rule I can raise a glass to," Duncan said to some groans.

The first consensus of the day was on who was going to buy drinks, Pete thought. How sadly appropriate.

The retreat was a casual session, so participants were free to get up and grab a coffee or pastry from the table set up in the small foyer outside the room. Richard wandered out with his empty coffee cup. About thirty seconds later a snappy calypso tune rang out from Jon's briefcase. The group laughed at Jon as he scrambled to open the case and checked the call display before shutting the device off in mid-steel-drum-beat.

"I'll have a beer," Duncan said.

"Make mine a double," Li said.

Drink orders came flowing in like last call in a college town. Just then Richard walked back into the room with a big grin on his face.

"You just called me, didn't you?" Jon asked Richard with a rueful smile.

"Yeah," Richard said, trying to hold in his glee. "I was wondering if you wanted cream in your coffee."

The group erupted in laughter.

"I'm glad to see hear a little laughter from all of you," Jason said. "Fun is something I didn't see enough of when I looked at your group. Your Laughter Index is pretty low. I *was* sent an e-mail from one of you with excellent moose-hunting advice for this session. The writer suggested three steps for us:

1. Stop picking up and throwing moose pies at each other and talk about the moose instead.
2. Agree to collectively jump up at the same time and tackle the moose when it appears, since any one individual will probably be killed if she/he tries it alone. Moose are really dangerous.
3. Figure out how the moose got in the room and block that path from any more of them getting in."

Jason finished the "getting started" section of the retreat by explaining the process they would be using to capture and sort out ideas. He handed out 3 x 5 inch yellow Post-it Notes and black fine-point felt pens. "We'll start with this Issues and Ideas parking lot," he said, tearing off a flip chart with that title and taping it onto a side wall. "Any issues you'd like to discuss or improvement ideas that come up, please write them on one of your Post-it Notes and stick it on this page."

To lay a foundation for their retreat, Jason led a short presentation and discussion on Navigating Change and balancing management and leadership. It was the same material he had covered in the workshop that Pete had attended and was in the book he handed out when they arrived. This time

Pete found the discussion of Navigator-Survivor-Victim and Pity City a lot more meaningful. He could see that he'd clearly slipped well below the line into pessimism and despair.

Jason asked the group for examples of victim-speak or statements of helplessness that they commonly heard at the office.

"The customer would never go for it," Duncan said.

"Corporate won't let us," Jon added.

"We've always done it that way," Richard said.

"We've never done it that way," someone else said.

"They don't understand," Li said.

"It's all ALIGN's fault and we can't do anything about it," Richard said, looking at Li.

She scowled.

"These statements may have a lot of truth in them," Jason said. "But being a Navigator – being a real leader – means framing the issues through what's possible. That calls for sorting out what we directly control, what we influence, and what we have no control over at all. Strong leaders don't 'awfulize' problems they have no control over. They accept those as 'it is what it is' and move on to the things they can control or influence."

It's time to become a Navigator again, Pete thought. Being a victim has eroded my enjoyment of life, my health, and my effectiveness in leading this team. It's hard to admit and it happened in such small bits. But I made the choice to put on my crap glasses for framing all the problems at work and at home. He thought about Michelle and the look in her eyes as she walked out the door. He was punishing the most important people in his life. She didn't marry the man he had become, and she deserved better.

The group jotted down their ideas on their Post-it Notes for how people they led could spend more time above the line.

These were added to the Issues and Ideas parking lot. The discussion moved on to balancing management and leadership.

"Management is seeing things as they are – what some might call reality," Jason explained. "Leadership is seeing things as they could be – the reality we want to create. We need both. We need to focus squarely on problems and we need to see the possibilities. It's a question of balance."

Jason then led the team through a balance-check exercise. At the end of the exercise, it was clear to everyone that the management team was so deeply involved in technical and management issues that there was very little time left for leadership.

It was the classic conflict: an endless stream of apparently urgent daily tasks successfully crowding out the more important strategic planning their roles required. They agreed that if the operations department's effectiveness was going to change, they would need to shift their focus toward more leadership activities. They did some more brainstorming with their Post-it Notes on ways the team could sharpen its leadership focus. Jason was soon tearing off additional flip-chart pages to accommodate the growing number of notes.

Then he moved the discussion to his findings. He passed out a copy of the report he had reviewed with Pete last week. He recapped how his conclusions were drawn from issues raised by staff focus groups, personal interviews with everyone in the room, and a management team e-mail survey. He had also reviewed the organizational survey with Heather.

"From all this, I've managed to identify the top operations department moose as communications, setting priorities, misaligned processes and systems, decision making, accountability, and leadership. Let's now look at the key point under each of these, starting with communications."

He went on to explain how communication is typically a catch-all term widely used for an array of organizational issues. In the operations department, he said, the single biggest communication problem was misuse of e-mail. He gave examples of "flaming e-mails" where the sparks of minor conflicts, feedback, smaller issues, and the like were fanned into roaring fires by cyberspace exchanges that should have been personal conversations. "I like to call the latter courageous conversations. They're difficult to have – especially if they've been uncomfortable or unsuccessful in the past. So people fire off an e-mail instead. That leads to the receiver replying in kind, which only makes the situation escalate."

"Yeah, I've sent and received a few of those," Zoë said.

"I guess those cowardly e-mails are the twigs and scrub brush that feed the moose," Richard said. Pete was glad to see a bit of Richard's humor returning.

"How do we deal with this problem?" Li asked.

This led to a discussion of the issue and ways of addressing it. The discussion concluded with an agreement that the team or a small task force needed to develop e-mail protocols for the group. The protocols would include when an e-mail was and wasn't appropriate, who should be copied on what e-mails, the length of e-mails, codes for levels of urgency, and ways of reviewing and reflecting on what was and wasn't working with the e-mail protocols. All these ideas were added to the Issues and Ideas parking lot.

Jason also identified ineffective meetings as a big source of communication problems. Pete winced, thinking back to Duncan and Richard's conversation a few weeks earlier. Jason discussed problems stemming from both the meeting process and behavior of attendees. One of the biggest holes in the process was the lack of clear agendas and advance planning concerning the who, what, when, where, or why of each item that was being discussed. He observed that operations department meetings generally had no ground rules or defined roles – such as time keeper or note taker. There was rarely any follow-up from previous meetings, and at the end of each discussion there was never any summary of what was decided or that defined any next steps.

The group asked for examples and Jason was well-primed to give them: late start times, sniping, put downs, potshots across the table at each other, constant interruptions by cell phones or visitors, cutting each other off, side conversations, not getting everyone's views on consensus decisions, and a few people having a meeting with everyone else just there as spectators.

The glum silence of the group indicated the truthfulness of his points. He also reported instances when most of the group felt a decision had been made, only to have others from the same meeting not support the decision and not pass it on to their own teams.

Jason aimed his next comment primarily at Pete. "One of the reasons your meetings are often ineffective, and a moose in its own right, is your team's decision-making process."

He went to explain how decisions are usually based on command, consultation, or consensus. "When it's not clear which type of method is being used, or who is making the decision, there's a lot of confusion and frustration."

He flashed a slide onto the screen that showed the three basic ways along a continuum for a team to make a decision:

Command – made by a team member (often the boss) without any input from other team members.

Consultative – made by a team member after consulting others who have knowledge or who must be committed to the decision for it to work.

Consensus – made by the entire team as a group.

Pete was beginning to understand that the further his team moved toward the consensus end of the continuum, the more buy-in or commitment there would be to decisions. Decision-making time may take a bit longer, but implementation time and effectiveness would dramatically improve.

Jason went on to speak about what he said was a common source of frustration and conflict in teams: when the decision-making method being used was not clear to everyone at the outset of the discussion. "Team leaders often add to the problem by leading what seems to be a consultative or even consensus discussion when they've already made up their minds."

Pete recognized this was the most common type of Doug meeting.

"This comes across as a 'guess what I am thinking' exercise. Or it can look like the leader is trying to manipulate the team into the 'right decision.' Some especially weak team leaders will intimidate team members into 'forced consensus' – now there's an oxymoron – and leave the discussion genuinely believing that the team was united in the decision."

"This is exactly what happens in so many of our meetings," Duncan said. "How can we fix it?"

"Pete and I conversed last week about these issues. It's not always easy for a leader to hear the truth, but he was very open to the coaching and feedback I offered. The meetings and decision-making moose are strongly linked to many of the leadership points I've listed in the next section. Let's review that section and then, Pete, this would be a good point for the group to give you feedback. Are you open for that?"

Pete's heart pounded and cold shivers shot up the backs of his legs. This leadership stuff is hard, he thought. For a second he considered how comfortable it was to sit on the line as a Survivor and wait for someone else to take action, while commiserating with all the other Victims in Pity City. It was so much easier when it's "them" and not "you" taking the hit for lack of leadership.

"Yeah, umm, sure," he said with a forced smile. "Wherever you feel it fits best."

After reviewing the leadership section, Jason said, "You'll have noticed by now that I like to gather input under the categories of keep doing, stop doing, and start doing. That's because these three questions help a team or an individual get the most balanced feedback. Please write the top three suggestions for each of these questions on your Post-it Notes for what you think Pete should keep doing, stop doing, and start doing."

After what seemed to Pete like hours of silence and furious writing, Jason gathered the notes for each category. With the group's help, he clustered the notes and put titles over each cluster.

The main clusters for "keep doing" were: Using Expertise/ Experience, Being Open to Feedback/Improvement, and Improvement Activities (Like This One).

Under "stop doing" were: Not Standing Up to Doug, Indecisiveness, Ineffective Meetings, and Priority Overload.

Under "start doing" were Set Clearer Priorities, More Delegating/Coaching, and Be More Positive/Strategic.

Pete went through each category, asking for clarity and examples. At first the team was reluctant and Jason had to prod them to go deeper. Eventually, clear stories and examples emerged, giving Pete a good sense of the advice his team was giving him. He felt drained when the discussion ended. If he was going to turn things around, he had a lot of work to do. But did he really want to?

During the afternoon break, Pete went for a solitary walk through the nature trails surrounding the lodge. He decided it was time to head back when he caught a glimpse through the trees near the marsh of a large brown animal with a huge rack of antlers. His stress beans weren't reducing his splitting headache one bit.

When he got back to the meeting room, two groups of three participants each had their chairs together in separate corners of the room. They were reviewing relevant sections of Jason's workbook for action ideas while brainstorming ways of dealing with the moose on their Post-it Notes. These were clustered and added to the many other flip-chart pages covering the walls.

Jason wrapped up the session by asking each participant for their personal reflections on the day. Most of the group was happy that some major issues were finally coming out, and that the discussions had been fairly frank and open. A few participants noted that zingers, barbs, and potshots were occasionally fired from around the room, but not as many as expected. There were even a few "bitch sessions" and the occasional "grump dump." But the main concern was that they felt in danger of being overwhelmed by the large number of issues and the hundreds of yellow notes now on the walls.

"How are we ever going to bring all this together?" Zoë asked. The others nodded in agreement.

After the session, Pete went back to his room to deal with some of the e-mails flooding his inbox before joining the group for a few Moosehead beers at the bar before dinner. The last e-mail he checked was from Doug, who sent a caustic update on NMTS's precarious financial situation. Apparently, the senior management team was considering whether to file for bankruptcy in order to get time to restructure the company financially.

Doug's closing line summed up his contempt for Pete's management exercise: "And I am quite sure the bankruptcy judge would not approve of jaunts into the woods while there's real work to be done here!"

As everyone finished their chocolate mousse desserts after dinner, Pete was given even more examples of issues within NMTS, operations, and his own leadership. In one conversation later in the evening, Jon expressed strong concerns to Pete about his use of pills and alcohol. Pete later hazily remembered assuring him there was nothing to worry about. However, as Pete's tongue tripped and slipped over each word, Jon had looked even more worried.

That night Pete engaged in another losing battle of trying to still his racing thoughts while he tossed and turned, trying to find a comfortable position for sleep. The sleeping pills weren't working – again. Pete slept fitfully as the day's discussions compounded with the other issues at home and work to create a blurry movie of doom. In one dream snippet, Amanda had formed an L on her forehead with the forefinger and thumb of her right hand. She kept mouthing the word "loser" to him.

Finally, at 4:07, he got out of bed and composed an e-mail to Doug. He'd had enough. It was his resignation. He went back to bed and slept soundly until the combination of alarm and wake-up call finally roused him.

Facing the Bull

Pete climbed groggily out of bed and shuffled into the bathroom to turn on the shower. His head felt like one of Alfred's arrows was stuck between his eyes. A grizzled, old man with a balloon face and tired, bloodshot eyes looked back at him from the mirror. Instinctively, he reached for the large pill bottle that was sitting right next to his toothbrush. He picked it up and gave it a shake. "Empty," he sighed, putting it back down. "I don't get it. I just opened that last night."

There was no magical rejuvenation for Pete in the shower. When he was younger he could stand in the shower for ages as the water battered his face. He loved it. But now, like a lot of things in life, it was just another thing he did to get the day started. Routine.

Drying himself off with the undersized towels – or were they really oversized facecloths? – Pete tried to imagine how he would explain quitting his job to Michelle. He groaned loudly. It's not like she was completely materialistic, but she hadn't taken a vow of poverty either. Quitting seemed like such a great idea a few hours ago. It sure took the pressure off. But it didn't really solve anything. Pete now had one more problem to deal with. "She'll leave me for sure," he said to the reflection peering glumly at him through the fogged-up mirror. "And what I am going to say to the team today when I cancel this retreat?"

It wasn't the first time Pete had talked to his reflection. He had started the strange ritual when he was a kid and felt lonely and helpless. And it was something he was doing more and more as he got older. "Maybe I should just call Jason's room and tell him to call off the session. I'll just slip away and go back and clean out my office. Or I could go meet with Doug and tell him it was a big impulsive mistake I made in the middle of the night after a few drinks. What's a little more groveling? It's not like I could go any lower."

Pete heard a rustling sound outside the bathroom and went to investigate. There, leaning against the TV cabinet, was Alfred. His lopsided grin morphed into a grimace at the sight of Pete's naked and dripping body.

"Yikes, big guy!" he said. "Don't do that to me so early in the morning. At least cover up your dangly parts."

Pete quickly backtracked and grabbed one of the tiny towels, wrapping as much of it around his waist as he could. He felt like he was back in the hospital wearing one of those moon gowns with southern exposure.

"Am I cursed with you for the rest of my life?" Pete stage-whispered to avoid being heard by anyone through the paper-thin walls. "How do I get rid of you? You're an incredibly persistent and really annoying elf delusion."

"Replace your liquid and pharmaceutical courage with the real thing and you'll never see me again."

Pete sat down hard on the bed and put his head in his hands. "I was going along and getting along okay until I woke up in this nightmare with you and all the moose."

"No, by running away from your toughest issues, you've been deluding yourself and sleepwalking for years. You're finally waking up."

Pete stared thoughtfully at the wall in front of him.

"In many ways you're like one of the two tramps in Samuel Beckett's play, *Waiting for Godot.*"

"Never heard of it."

"Two tramps are waiting by a sickly-looking tree for the arrival of M. Godot. We never learn who Godot is or why he's important. The tramps quarrel, make up, contemplate suicide, try to sleep, eat a carrot, and gnaw on some chicken bones. Two other characters appear: a cruel master and his slave. The master claims to own the land they are on and has his slave entertain them. A young boy arrives to say that M. Godot will not come today, but that he will come tomorrow. The play ends with one tramp saying to the other, 'Well? Shall we go?' 'Yes, let's go,' replies the other tramp. They do not move. The curtain comes down."

Pete was deep in thought as he gingerly retrieved his clothes and backed into the bathroom to put them on.

"Godot isn't coming," Alfred shouted. "Stop putting in time on Helpless Highway. Get out of Pity City! You've got to face your issues and move your life forward."

Pete walked out of the bathroom, buttoning his shirt. "You know, Alfred, I *am* sick of going along to get along. I *want* more courage. I *need* more courage. But courage is much easier to talk about than find."

"You're a Leonard – a brave heart! You already have it. You just need to regain control of your fear. It's in you already. Follow your heart."

Alfred fell backwards into the bed and put his hands behind his head. "So what *would* you do if you weren't afraid?" he asked.

"I'd go into today's meeting and flesh out all the feedback and priorities that come from the team. Then I'd make them happen."

"Tally ho! So go do it!"

"Even if I wanted to, I screwed up those plans by sending Doug my resignation e-mail a few hours ago. I guess I am running away again."

"Actually, Elric called in a favor from the cyber gods and zapped your e-mail. It never got to Doug. In fact, it's not even on your computer any more. It never happened."

"Who's Elric?"

"He's my boss. It's an Old English name that means elf ruler. He is ..."

Pete rushed out of the room, slamming the door behind him.

The early-morning sun looked like it just might break through the hazy mist. The long dreary days of heavy rain were finally ending. Pete paused and took a few gulps of clean, fresh air. It was filled with that heady spring promise of warm summer days ahead. Crocuses and daffodils cheerily waved to him as he stepped onto the wooden bridge spanning the swollen and fast-running creek and leading to the log conference building.

Considering his tough night, he felt surprisingly good. Pete couldn't remember the last time he was filled with this much energy. His mind was clear and churning over all that needed to be done. With a hearty chuckle he saluted a large bull moose standing and drinking water downstream in the creek. The moose raised its mouth quickly and snorted menacingly as water streamed off the huge fur bell hanging from its throat.

A continental breakfast was spread out on the table at the back of the room. Pete called out a good morning to Jason and helped himself to the succulent fresh fruit and a large golden muffin. It was still early and Jason was the only other person in the room. He was munching on a bagel and fruit, reviewing his notes. Occasionally he would wander up to one of the flip charts on the wall and read over some of the notes and transcribe some of them onto his pad.

"You sound cheery today, Pete," he said.

"I'm not really sure why, but I actually feel invigorated. Yesterday was tough. I was just about ready to throw in the towel last night. But I think I'm finally getting what you, this team, and a certain klutzy advisor are saying to me. I'm sick and tired of going along to get along. Believe it or not, I was once a very strong leader just as you've outlined in your books and presentations."

"So I've heard."

"I don't know what happened. It was all so gradual. As each little issue or problem came along, it never seemed like it was worth making a big deal of. But I slowly lost control of my time and my life. Good old Doug, our customers, my peers, members of the team, and the crazy-busy world of meetings, e-mails, and phone calls just ground me down. I slipped deeper and deeper below the line. I hate to admit it, but I was one of those helpless victims you talk about. I've been living in a pill-popping, alcoholic haze for way too long. It's like I've been dozing through the last fifteen years of my life."

"I think you're being a little too hard on yourself."

"No, actually I haven't been hard enough on myself. That's been the problem. Well, no more! It's time to take the moose by the tail and face the situation."

Pete tried to ignore the sharp snort over his left shoulder and the hot breath on the back of his neck.

"Winston Churchill once said, 'The courage to look hard realities in the face is essential to effective leadership,'" Jason said. "I am glad to hear you're ready to do that. This could be a real breakthrough retreat for you and your department if you truly follow through on what you're saying."

"Mornin'," Duncan muttered as he shuffled into the room. His brown hair was unusually disheveled. He looked tired and gloomy. The rest of the team straggled in over the next twenty minutes. They didn't look much better than Duncan. While they mumbled to each other and picked at their breakfasts, Pete pieced together that most of them had stayed up a lot later than he had, drinking and commiserating. Heather was the only one looking bright and chipper. As an outsider to the team and part of corporate, she'd been deliberately – though unusually – quiet during the entire retreat and hadn't mixed much with the participants.

After a few more minutes of private conversation with Jason in the foyer, Pete started the meeting.

"Good morning, everyone. I'd like to start by thanking you for all your honesty and openness yesterday in naming the moose we need to deal with. I'm glad to see that the conversations you all had with Jason before this retreat were open and honest. I'd especially like to thank you for yesterday's frank and helpful input."

Pete pointed to the flip charts on the wall with Post-it Notes clustered under Keep Doing, Stop Doing, and Start Doing. "I haven't been receptive to feedback like this over the past few years, so last night was really tough for me."

He was surprised – and pleased – to see Alfred leaning in the doorframe, smiling.

"If you can believe it, I actually put together a resignation e-mail for Doug early this morning."

Richard and Duncan glanced at each other with eyebrows raised. Zoë looked a little startled and concerned.

"Very fortunately, a technical glitch saved me from myself and it was wiped off my computer before it got through to him."

Alfred grinned and gave Pete a quick "you're welcome" bob of his head, making the long black and white feather on his hat quiver wildly.

"I know it sounds like an empty promise – even a worn-out cliché – but this is a whole new day for me. And I intend to make it the start of a whole new era for this team. I'm ready, willing, and I believe able to turn things around. Jason, let's get started."

As Pete sat down, he scanned the group and noted that they were more awake than a few minutes earlier.

The first agenda item was team visioning. Jason led the group through a guided imagery exercise to imagine operations a few years down the road, when the moose issues and improvement ideas discussed yesterday were successfully implemented. "As you make notes on your personal picture, each of you is developing a series of stained-glass pieces that we'll pull together to paint the mural of the preferred future for operations," he said.

Over the next hour, energy levels rose sharply as the team's collective picture merged into a strong consensus. They wanted an organization with high levels of customer satisfaction, energized and involved team members at all levels, and a "leaderful organization" (based on yesterday's definition of leadership as action, not a position). They talked about how in such an organization everyone would take strong initiative and ownership, would show lots of openness and trust, and would work together to break down departmental silos/barriers.

"We'll never again hear 'that's my not my job' or 'that's not my department,'" Zoë said.

The group dreamed about highly streamlined processes with dramatically fewer errors and much faster turnaround times, and soaring morale levels.

They also agreed on the desirability of aligned systems and structure. "That's where you're going to have to step up, Pete," Li said. "We don't control things like ALIGN or the problems we have with disconnects between our department and others."

"I'm as sick of being a helpless victim on these issues as you are," Pete said. "With your input and suggestions on where the highest leverage will come from, I'm ready to tackle the corporate moose."

Alfred gave him a thumbs up and slight tip of his feathery hat from the doorway.

"So as we look back at the picture of your preferred future that's emerged here, what are your reflections?" Jason asked, pointing to the flip charts with all of the group's notes clustered and categorized together.

"I am quite surprised and very encouraged by just how much we agree on where we want to lead operations," Richard said. Others chimed in with similar comments.

"I know Cy would be delighted to see the alignment between where you want to take operations and what needs to happen corporately," Heather said.

"Okay, so we've all held hands and dreamed big dreams," Duncan cut in with a smirk. "What's next? A group hug and singing Kum Ba Ya?" A few people chuckled. "I hate to rain on your parade, people. But there's an unbridgeable gulf between this fantasy world and the cold hard reality of operations and NMTS."

"Looks like Duncan is on the Bitter Bus to Pity City for a big old Pity Party," Richard said.

"Duncan makes an excellent point," Pete said. "We need to put solid plans in place to move us forward. Jason, I believe that's what you're planning to guide us through next."

"Absolutely. Let's take a break and come back to develop your strategic imperatives."

During the break, Pete observed that most of the participants were livelier and more animated than when the day began. Duncan approached him with his concerns about the futility of this exercise when there were so many pressing issues and decisions the team needed to make right now. Pete asked him to hold off until the end of the day to see how the whole process was unfolding. Duncan reluctantly agreed.

When they returned, Jason said, "A strategic imperative is a project or initiative that is very high leverage – or strategic and a must-do – an imperative – to move operations much closer to the vision you've all just put together. Usually they have a one-year time frame. Given the pressing urgency of what's happening at NMTS, and especially within operations, you likely want to focus your efforts on the next three to six months."

Jason paused to let that sink in. "Take a look at the report I gave you yesterday and the ideas we've put on all the walls around us. We're going to start by brainstorming a list of possible imperatives and then cluster them until we have three to five strategic imperatives. Too many teams get caught up in long lists of urgencies and top priorities. I have seen as many as thirty-five to forty 'must do' projects paralyzing an organization with conflicting goals and priorities."

"We could probably top that," Li said.

Pete had a painful flashback to Doug's management meeting with Omar's strong argument for that team to set clearer priorities and Doug's refusal to take anything off their long to-do list. It was all critically – and impossibly – important to Doug. That was clearly one of the key reasons that Damali had resigned.

Over the next thirty minutes, Jason recorded ideas for operations' strategic imperatives on a few flip charts. He then guided everyone through an exercise he called "bucketing" – grouping similar ideas. After a lively debate, they put headings on all eight clusters. Jason then led them through a voting process to prioritize imperatives in order to shrink the list to five or less.

The imperative with the most votes was Culture Change/ Leadership Development (this included reducing victim thinking, bringing core values to life, increasing teamwork/ownership, and developing leadership skills at all levels).

This was followed closely by Process Management (reducing costly errors and rework, improving client service levels, and breaking down departmental silos), which was almost tied with Communications (increasing two-way conversations up, down, and across operations; identifying and dealing with moose issues; and using e-mail more effectively).

Decision Making and Accountability (cutting bureaucracy by reducing approval levels/bottlenecks, simplifying systems, and getting everyone to take more responsibility for their work) created quite a bit of debate and discussion about cause and effect and to what extent operations could control or influence some aspects of this issue.

The last cluster rounding out their top five was Management Team Dynamics (increasing meeting effectiveness, reducing turf protection, and increasing teamwork and coordination).

"I'd say we've had a great morning," Pete said as they prepared to break for lunch. Heads nodded in agreement around
the room. Duncan shrugged slightly, but looked more hopeful.
"Let's have lunch so we can get into the details this afternoon,"
Pete said. "We've got to set action plans if we're going to implement these imperatives."

Pete stayed behind to review the notes and reflect on what
he needed to do to in order to lead the charge forward. As he
walked out to get a bit of fresh air, Alfred appeared beside him.

"Welcome back to the world of brave hearts, Mr. Leonard!"
he said. "It's great to see you reawakening your leader within!"
He clamped his arm around Pete's neck and pounded him
hard on his left shoulder.

"Ow! I appreciate your support," Pete said rubbing his
shoulder. "But I wish you'd be less physical with your enthu-
siasm. It really does feel great to be a Navigator again. For the
first time in a long while I feel like I might be in control. I am
pumped about where we can go with all this. I didn't realize
how much I'd missed the land of the living."

"You're off to a great start. But of course the real work has
yet to begin." Alfred's face grew solemn. "There's something
very serious brewing with all the moose in your office and
even around this lodge," he said. "Word of your awakening is
out, and the moose are acting threatened and becoming very
agitated. And a threatened moose can be a deadly moose. I'll
try to stay close to help with this the best as I can, but I'd feel
a whole lot better if we could figure out why my arrows have
no effect on them."

After lunch the group took each of the strategic imperatives and
identified a team leader from around the management table for
each one. Pete took on Management Team Effectiveness and

joined the Decision Making and Accountability team led by Jon to help with the corporate issues they would encounter.

Each team leader then led a discussion, getting input from everyone about who from operations (and some from outside the division in corporate services such as finance, IT, and HR) would be best suited to join each team. The leaders also discussed the scope and mandate of their team, what outcomes were expected, and rough time frames. Everyone agreed they would get back together with Jason for a follow-up session in four weeks.

As they wrapped up the session, Jason went around the table to gather reflections from each participant. Duncan started off. "Well, as most of you know, I was not in favor of this retreat. This whole Moose-on-the-Table thing was just a little too cute. I thought it was a waste of time given all that we need to be doing. Some of Jason's approaches felt a little too smooth and theoretical. He seemed slicker than moose guts on a doorknob."

"Eeeeyyyuuu," Zoë said.

Duncan grinned and continued. "I was convinced we'd see that he really put the con in conference." A few people groaned. "But I am pleasantly surprised by what I've heard here. And I'm really surprised how you've responded with the leadership you seem to be showing, Pete."

Pete smiled and nodded his thanks.

"The big test will be when we get back to the swamp," Duncan said. "Will we follow through on all these plans and good intentions? I guess we'll just have to see."

Everyone nodded, and the rest of the comments were even more positive and hopeful.

"I want to thank you all for your active and candid participation," Pete said in his closing remarks. "I've been head of this team for a while now, but I'll admit I haven't been much of a leader. If courage was money, I'd have had a hard time paying for a coffee. But I'll commit to you that you're going to see a very different set of behaviors from me from now on. Jason is going to have all these notes typed up and e-mailed to us within the next week. I am going to study your feedback to me and work hard to act on it. When I stumble, I hope you'll all feel free to call me on it. Of course, I also appreciate feedback on my successes too. So let's go do it!"

The atmosphere in the meeting room was the warmest and most energized Pete could ever remember. Many people lingered and seemed reluctant to leave, even though they had a long drive ahead of them.

Pete's car was parked near his cabin on the other side of the lodge property. He strode energetically toward it in the warm spring sunshine He thought about the long drive home. Would Michelle be there? He contemplated just how much work was ahead and how keen he was to get started.

As he neared his car, he heard a bellow and a clattering behind him. Pete turned and froze in terror. The huge bull moose he had seen in the creek that morning was charging at full gallop with his massive rack of antlers aimed straight for Pete's midsection. He was about thirty feet away and closing fast. Pete tightened with panic. There was nowhere to run. Nowhere to hide. He was going to be squished against his car like a fat juicy June bug.

Pete heard a shrill whistling sound over his left shoulder. Abruptly the bull moose stumbled, fell, and plowed head first into the gravel. An arrow protruded from the bull's large chest. Bright red blood quickly colored the brown fur and gushed across the gravel. Pete looked behind him to see Alfred on the raised log porch just in front of Pete's cabin door in a sideways archer stance with his legs spread wide. Alfred lowered his great longbow with a look of relief. Pete turned back to the bull moose.

Which slowly faded, vaporized into thin air, and was gone.

Two Steps Forward,
Four Hooves Back

Pete could feel his blood pressure rise as he quickly scanned the e-mail conversation thread on his computer. This was the third round in a series of finger-pointing e-mails between Li and Richard that he'd been copied on. The cyber fur was flying. The accusations, emotions, and rhetoric were escalating. In the past he would have let them duke this out on their own. But this was a new era, and Pete knew it was time for him to do some conflict resolution and coaching.

Halfway through the first line of his response, he stopped. Wait a minute, he thought. This is exactly the kind of situation our e-mail protocol group addressed. Things have clearly escalated beyond anything an e-mail would fix. I need to get them together.

He deleted his e-mail response and phoned Li and Richard directly to arrange a meeting in his office that afternoon. Pete pulled out an old training manual to brush up on the key steps for resolving conflict.

It was a rocky meeting. Getting Li and Richard to find common ground and areas of agreement took some time. They kept putting each other down for the bad intentions and poor attitudes they saw in each other. Pete continually had to bring them back to the basic ground rule of "focusing on the situation, issue, or behavior and not the person." This rule was one of several take-aways from Jason's retreat that was helping make the team's meetings much more effective.

By the end of the meeting, they'd agreed that the core of the issue was really a problem with operations' work order and dispatching process. It was riddled with errors.

This was one of the key strategic imperatives that Li's Process Management team had been working on since the retreat three weeks ago. The process errors created misinformation, incomplete work orders, and disjointed records. Staff members in both Li and Richard's areas believed the other group was just being sloppy and uncommunicative, or didn't care about customers and work quality. The people involved were symptom carriers for the deeper process problems.

Li and Richard didn't exactly hug each other and become best friends, but Pete helped them see the roots of the issue and look for ways to focus the discussion on facts and analysis rather than personalities. Richard – and Pete – also saw a whole new dimension to the Process Management team, and why it was so critical for Li to have her best and most knowledgeable staff members involved in the mapping and improvement effort.

Those three weeks following the retreat were hectic. In fact, nothing had really changed. However, Pete's overall temperament and awareness of how he was using his time, what was happening within his team, and what needed to be done to move operations beyond the swampy bog filled with moose, improved dramatically. These changes were also reflected at home. Michelle – while still frustrated with Pete and their marriage – had at least moved back home, hoping things would get better.

One of the most noticeable changes in operations showed up in their weekly meetings. Pete completely rethought, and talked with the team about, what they wanted to get out of these few hours together each week. They agreed that information updates should be handled electronically and be kept to very brief mentions when they were together. The main thing they needed to do when together was resolve issues or problems – especially those that crossed department lines or were division wide.

Just as importantly, they agreed to a strategy of "follow-through and follow-up" on plans and commitments made to each other. Clarifying each agenda item and deciding whether any decisions they were making would be done by command, consultation, or consensus dramatically sharpened and focused their discussions.

"Thanks, Richard. It sounds like you're right on track," Pete said as he joined the applause following Richard's hour-long discussion and update on the progress of his Strategic Imperative team.

"I really like how your team is involving key people from other departments and digging down to get at the roots of the issue," Li added.

"Thanks. I'm glad we're on the same page on this one," Richard said with a smile.

"Wow! I'm impressed," Jason said. He was there for one of his occasional coaching sessions. "I don't know if I've ever seen a team make so much progress so quickly. It's been only five weeks since our Elkhorn retreat and the amount of co-operation and discipline in your meetings is quite remarkable."

"Yeah, who'd have thought we'd have our old Pete back to get us to this point?" Duncan said. "Seriously, you've helped us all to focus on what needs to get done. You might even make a believer out of this crusty old guy. Our meetings used to be like moose horns – a point here and a point there and a whole lot of bull in between. Now we get right to the issues and set action plans."

Richard chimed in with, "I used to think that our meetings were a bloody interruption to my work. Now I see how they are a key part of our leadership work and can get us all pulling together more effectively. I never thought I'd say this, but these meetings are becoming the highlight of my week. Maybe that shows I *really* need to get a life."

"Well, Jon, you're up," Jason said. "How are things with the Decision Making and Accountability team you've put together?"

Jon led a lively discussion outlining how his team was analyzing the root causes of this complex issue to sort out the process, system, skill, and organizational culture components. "We've concluded that part of our problem is rooted in corporate issues, especially how decisions and follow-through are handled by Doug's team. We all know this is a very touchy and tough issue for Pete to take on. We're arming him with data and facts as well as solid examples to help him get changes made with Doug and that team."

"How are you feeling about that?" Jason asked Pete.

"It's not a conversation I'm exactly looking forward to," Pete said. "But I know it's vital to moving us forward on this critical imperative."

"They sure are a Sunflower Team," Jon said.

"What's that mean?" Zoë asked.

"Sunflower Teams always turn toward the boss for enlightenment. From what I understand, Doug is such a hard-ass he makes Attila the Hun look like Mother Teresa. I've heard he's the biggest bully moose in the company. I wouldn't want to be you right now, Pete."

For a fleeting moment Pete didn't want to be Pete either. "I'll deal with Doug," he said. "Here's my chance to sharpen my *upward* leadership skills."

"… and for the leader of the Mickey Moose Club, here's a special T-shirt, vest, and hat," Duncan said. The shirt featured a moose head caricature, antlers curled into three sections like Mickey Mouse's head and ears, with a big bushy "moose-tache" drawn on the creature's upper lip.

Pete slipped the shirt on. Then he put on the florescent orange hunting vest and red plaid hunting hat.

Someone suggested he wear the outfit to his meeting with Doug the next morning. Everyone laughed and a few people applauded.

The operations management team had driven across town to have lunch at The Moose in a Caboose, a quirky restaurant featuring a train caboose inside an abandoned train station that had supposedly been revamped as a northern hunting lodge. It was replete with moose and hunting paraphernalia. The wall of oversized televisions was always on, making it a very popular spot to watch hockey, baseball, or whatever other sport was in season. The menu featured moose-links sausage, moose burgers, and moose steaks. The team was celebrating the progress they'd made in the two months since their Elkhorn Lodge retreat.

"And here are some moose droppings to remind us to always watch out for signs of moose and be ready to deal with all the crap still going on within the company," Zoë said. She handed out plastic bags containing a few large clusters of nuts, caramel nougat, and dried fruit held together by milk chocolate.

"Let's toast our chief moose hunter," Jon said as he raised a moose mug of the house draft – Swamp Water Dark Ale.

"I'll certainly drink to that," Heather said. "The other corporate HR people and I are hearing and seeing many promising signs that morale may be on the upswing in operations. I'm happy to say that the news has made its way up to Cy, and he's asked me to put this event on our tab as a way of saying thanks for everything you guys are doing."

Once the clapping died down, she continued, "I was doing a little online research yesterday – on my break, of course." Laughter rippled around the large table. "Someone speculated that the Moose-on-the-Table metaphor originated from an actual incident in Maine on a very hot summer day during a garden wedding reception. According to the story, a very sick baby moose crawled under a large skirted buffet table and died. It created a horrid stench. No one knew the origin of the smell, and given the formality of the reception, nobody mentioned it. Everyone tried to carry on as if there was no problem. Meanwhile, guests were heading to the restrooms and becoming ill as the odor spread."

Pete noticed Alfred sitting up on the crude-cut wooden rafters above the far end of their table. He was scowling as he pinched his nose and shook his bare head.

"But that would be a moose *under* the table," Duncan said.

"Can we *please* change the subject?" Zoë said. "This isn't the kind of discussion I want to have just before I taste my first moose burger."

They went on to talk about the progress each Strategic Imperative team was making. As Pete listened to the various conversations going on around the table, he reflected on how much higher people's energy levels were and how much better he was feeling. He wasn't even sure when he'd last taken a pill. And things were improving at home between him and Michelle too.

As everyone was getting up to go back to the office, Jon said, "It's funny, but my five-year-old daughter's favorite bedtime story is *If You Give a Moose a Muffin*. I read it to her for about the tenth time last night. The story involves a mannerly moose who smells something good. He's invited in for a muffin. But then he eats all of them. Then the huge visitor wants you to make more. And since you are out of ingredients, he wants to go shopping with you. It's really cold outside. So the big suck wants a sweater. Getting him one leads to a puppet show and a huge mess. As they clean up, he notices berries. This reminds him of muffins and so ..."

"That sounds a lot like what was happening in our team," Li said. "We were feeding the moose, which then led to more and more complications and moose adventures – pun intended."

"Exactly," Jon said. "That's what I was thinking as I read the story again last night."

Pete saw Alfred high above the table nodding his blond head. What happened to his feathery hat? he wondered.

"So why didn't I hear any plans to deal with the 'clockroaches' around here?" Doug was in fine fighting form. He leaned forward with both elbows on the conference table and stared disdainfully at his management team. His walrus moustache was quivering. Scribbled notes, coffee cups, and the floor all became fascinating points of interest for every-one around the table.

A few days ago Doug had sent all his managers an e-mail with the subject line, "Kill the Clockroaches!!" The e-mail was about the company's growing absenteeism problem. The main part of the message read:

> *Clockroaches are those employees who are as useful as a roach and mooch off of our time clock. Judging by the parking lot at starting and quitting times, we have way too many Clockroaches around here. I am fed up with you telling me about their excuses, whining, and complaining. We need a new standard for you and them: impress me or leave.*

Doug went on in the message to outline tough new atten-dance rules he expected managers to enforce. He closed the e-mail with an order for each manager to send a "clockroach management plan" to him immediately.

"I don't think calling our staff clockroaches is consistent with NMTS's value of treating each other with respect," Pete said softly. He was sitting straight up in his chair with both hands resting on the table in front of him. He looked calmly and steadily at Doug.

"Oh, that's rich, coming from you, Leonard!" Doug low-ered his head and raised his eyes menacingly.

Pete could have sworn he heard a snort and the pawing of a big hoof. Doug's double chin quivered and Pete thought he caught a fleeting glimpse of a fur bell.

"Your operations department has missed every number and commitment you've ever been given," Doug said. "So your credibility to spout values at me is about nil. You run the loosest ship we have around here. Where's the respect for our customers and the rest of this company in that? Huh? *Huh?* So what do you do while our company's problems are growing? You take your managers off on a two-day vacation to some hunting lodge. Then you all come back here spewing gibberish about moose that causes your own staff – and even people from other departments – to get out of real work by attending pointless meetings! A whole room full of clockroaches!"

"We're making some real progress in getting to the root cause of many of our problems ..."

"I am looking at the root cause of many of operations' problems!"

Pete heard Rosie inhale as if getting ready to absorb a punch. He felt an old – way too old – and familiar rush of energy and resolve. Doug can only bully me with my permission, he thought. And I refuse to give him that power.

"Doug, I don't think this is the time or place to have this discussion. I'll brief you on what we've been doing at our meeting tomorrow ..."

"It better be good, Leonard! I can see *this* meeting is going to be a waste of time. Get back to work everybody!" Doug stormed out of the room. Rhonda gave a perplexed look to the group, closed her computer, quickly gathered up her things, and followed him out the door.

Everyone sat in stunned silence. Finally Rosie gave a nervous laugh and said, "Well, that went well. What did you think, Pete?"

"No, Rosie, that didn't go quite as well as it could have," Pete replied with a chuckle. Nervous laughter broke some of the tension in the room.

"Doug is about as subtle as a flashing neon sign in a diner window," Chuck added. "But underneath that blustery exterior is an enormous lack of character."

"Maybe he should try switching to decaf," Rosie suggested.

"What's going on in operations?" Omar asked. "I'm hearing a lot of good things from my folks in IT."

"Well, since this meeting was so short and we've all sched-uled an hour into our day anyway, do you want to hear about our Strategic Imperative teams?" Pete asked. "I was hoping to do that at our next meeting after I talked to Doug. A fair bit of our work is going to impact your departments too. And the more we work together, the better off the whole division will be."

"Absolutely," Harold said. "It's great to have the old Pete Leonard back. Let's hear what you've all been up to and how we can get involved."

Everyone around the table nodded in agreement.

After Pete commented on all the work under way in oper-ations, he was given a few good suggestions for rounding out some of the teams – especially Process Management, Communications, and Decision Making and Accountability – with stronger cross-departmental representation. Each man-ager volunteered a few staff names from their own department.

"People in our sales group are noticing quite a change in operations," Chuck said. "I can see now that you're killing off a few moose and liberating everyone."

Ever since returning from Elkhorn Lodge – and Alfred's dramatic kill of the big bull moose – Pete had noticed that the moose around operations were getting weaker and weaker. Many had disappeared completely.

"I don't envy your meeting tomorrow morning with Doug," Omar said.

"I think I saw antlers sprouting from Doug's head," Rosie said with a laugh.

As he drove home, Pete was lost in thought about his upcoming meeting with Doug. As he sat waiting at a red light, the words of the Alanis Morissette song playing on the radio jolted him back to reality: "For the ocean is big and my boat is small. Find the courage."

The Last Re-snort

Pete nervously made his way past Rhonda's desk toward Doug's large, luxurious office. Before Doug joined the company, it was actually a board room. As Pete moved past Rhonda, he was startled to see spindly moose legs and large hoofs where her legs should have been.

Doug's office was filled with expensive antique reproduction furniture. Adding to the elaborate décor was rosewood inlaid flooring and a thick oval Persian rug covering much of the center of the room. The large phony wood grain sign garishly declaring "Doug Drake – Senior Vice President" was badly out of place on his mahogany desk.

Doug's oversized brown leatherette – "genuine vinyl" – chair was facing away from Pete as he entered the office. The chair swiveled around toward him. Pete gasped and drew in a sharp breath. Doug had a huge rack of antlers growing from his head. As Pete watched in horror, Doug's large round face morphed slowly into a huge moose head. Doug – or the moose – started to snort heavily with bursts of steam blasting from each nostril. His antlers scraped the white stucco ceiling as the biggest, hairiest, and brawniest bull moose Pete had ever seen rose from the chair.

The moose lowered his massive antlers. With one step forward he pinned Pete against the wood-paneled office wall. Rhonda was standing at the door giggling like a little school girl excitedly clapping two large hoofs together at the end of her hairy brown legs. Pete felt the powerful pressure of the antlers crushing him. He couldn't breathe against the excruciating pain …

Pete awoke with a start. Painful contractions were shooting through his chest. He was drenched in sweat. What a vivid dream, he thought. Michelle was breathing rhythmically as she slept beside him. Pete walked quietly to the bathroom. He opened the medicine cabinet and saw the bottle. He gave it a quick shake and was happy to know it was still half full. He hadn't had a pill in a few weeks and hadn't been sure there were any left. He popped a couple into his mouth and washed them down with glass of water. After a couple of deep breaths, he began to feel better.

Yawning and scratching himself, he walked back to bed. In the darkness, he saw something on his pillow. He assumed it was Michelle, shifting over to take advantage of the extra room. Still groggy, he reached out to gently shift her over. But if it was Michelle, she'd suddenly become very hairy. Pete flicked on the lamp and was paralyzed with fear. He tried to scream, but there was no sound. On his pillow was the massive bull moose head and antlers he'd just dreamed about. Bright red blood oozed from its severed neck, coloring his pillow and pooling on the sky blue bedsheets. Pete bellowed, but still couldn't force out any sound as he backed away from the bed. He smashed into the dresser and cracked his head against the mirror, shattering the glass.

"Pete, Pete, honey, it's okay! Calm down. You'll be all right."

Pete found himself sitting up in bed. Michelle had her left arm around his shoulder and was worriedly caressing his face with her right hand.

"I just had an incredible set of nightmares," Pete whispered shakily. "They were so vivid and real."

The red numbers of the clock radio showed 5:43.

As Pete retold Michelle the details of his dreams, they seemed more and more ridiculous to him. How could they have frightened him? Morphing bosses and an homage to *The Godfather*? Ridiculous.

They decided they might as well get up and have breakfast. As they drank their coffee, Michelle said, "In the past few weeks I've seen the authentic guy I married returning again. You're the hero of this story on your 'road of trials,' as Joseph Campbell described it in his research on our ancient and modern mythologies and stories."

Pete smiled at his wife's teacherly tone. "Any encounter with Doug is a *trial*, all right, but I sure don't feel like a hero," he said.

"What's the worst that can happen today as a result of talking to Doug?"

"I could be fired and we'll lose this house."

"I'm into drama, but you're the one overacting now. We won't lose the house. We have some money saved and you're a very employable guy – especially if you keep the positive mindset of the last month or so. Doug can't come between us. He can't take away your family. Without your permission, he can't take away your dignity and self-respect. He might alter your journey in the short term – but ultimately he can't destroy your future."

Pete nodded slowly.

"As you know, I'm developing an interest in the roots or origins of names," Michelle said. "So last night I did a little research on Doug Drake. Doug is an anglicized form of a Gaelic name meaning 'dark river' or 'blood river.' One of the possible beginnings of his name is from an Old English word meaning dragon. So maybe he's the dragon guarding the bridge over the dark river. And you have to face him on your road of trials!"

Pete gave Michelle a puzzled look. "You're into names too? Next thing you'll be saying 'tally ho.'"

"Leonard, I didn't appreciate you embarrassing me in the meeting yesterday," Doug snapped. "Your insubordination was *%#_^ unacceptable!"

"I'm sorry if you felt embarrassed – that certainly was not my intent," Pete replied. "We have a serious morale crisis and it clearly comes from a large we/they gap that's grown up between managers and front-line staff. I believe all of us in management positions need to be careful about the language we use to describe other departments, each other, and staff. Words are powerful and create our worlds."

The butterflies in Pete's stomach were still fluttering around. But his old energy and resolve were returning. He had decided to withdraw his agreement to let Doug intimidate him. He would somehow manage to get the butterflies flying in formation.

"Well, I expect you to be more of a team player and not argue with me in front of the rest of my team."

"I agree completely," Pete said. "We don't need arguing within the management team. But we could use many more healthy debates both in my own team and in your management group." He was feeling stronger by the word. "We actually need *a lot more* debate. We all need to air key issues, examine differing points of view, and understand each other's perceptions."

"We do that now."

"I have found that too many of the real discussions in the operations team happened in the hallway *after* our meetings. And I've been part of those same conversations after the management team meetings."

Pete refrained from calling them "your management meetings." No need to poke a bull moose in the eye with a sharp stick, he thought. "We've got to find ways to bring those conversations back into the meeting room if we're going to get to the root causes of the problems that are slowing choking this company."

"Leonard, get off all that soft group-hug crap! This isn't a democracy. Our problems are weak and indecisive leadership like yours. We need less team building and more action. Our bankers visited Cy and me last week to review last month's financial statements. Their patience – and money to prop us up – is running out. *Fast!*"

Pete was determined not to let Doug sidetrack the conversation with personal attacks and bully tactics. "Doug, the main reason I asked for this meeting was to brief you on the work we're doing in operations and what we need from you and the management team to turn things around. Should we get into that now?"

"Okay. Shoot."

Now there's a real temptation on my road of trials, Pete thought. He told Doug he wanted to spend some time reviewing the process his team had been through since the Elkhorn Lodge retreat.

"Ah, yes. Your expensive little jaunt in the northern woods to escape reality," Doug said.

Pete ignored the comment. Throughout his summary, he handed Doug briefing notes on what each Strategic Imperative team was working on and the progress they were making. Doug yawned a few times and looked out his window. From time to time he refreshed his e-mail screen, glancing at messages as they popped up.

"Now we get to the team that really needs some help from you, your management group, and other departments," Pete said. "Jon and his team have done an excellent job of analyzing the roots of our decision making and accountability challenges."

Doug wasn't exactly all ears. "Ah yes. This is the 'let's blame our problems on others' group. A strong offense is always the best defense, isn't it? Let's point at them so people don't look at us."

"Not quite," Pete said calmly. "We're trying to get at the deeper, systemic roots of this issue. Decision making and accountability have been a continual problem throughout our company because we've tended to look for *who* to blame rather than *what* it is about our interconnected systems, processes, or even our structure that is keeping us from being effective. Our departmental silos, disjointed procedures, and even our performance management system, which is focused on our individual performance and incentives, have us knotted in a big ball of intertwined problems. Let me show you some excellent data and trend analysis that Jon's team has pulled together along with their recommend—"

"All right, Leonard. Enough! I've been very patient – way too patient. The work your teams are doing *might* have some long-term value. But we don't have long term. Our issues are immediate. What *%#_^ part of that do you not understand? How can I make this any clearer for you? I want you to stop wasting all this *%#_^ time on your *teams* and get everyone focused on fixing operations – *now*! You don't need all this bullshit analysis and planning. I can tell you right now what your problems are if you don't know them already. You need action. Do I make myself clear?"

Pete felt his heart rate spiking. "I understand where you're coming from. I have a very strong sense of urgency about fixing these issues. It's also become very clear to me that our problems need much deeper and more thoughtful solutions than the half-baked actions we've been throwing at them. That's why they never go away. We've been taking painkillers to get rid of the symptoms. But we really need to diagnose and treat the cause of our sickness. That means—"

"For god's sake, Leonard. Enough with all the excuses and stalling. Give me a real action plan by four this afternoon or clean out your office!"

"So how was your meeting with Doug?" Jon asked anxiously. "Did he go for any of our recommendations?"

"It didn't go well. He hasn't been part of the process and learning we've been through over the past few months, so he doesn't understand the convoluted mess that our core operating and decision-making processes have become. He's under a lot of pressure to turn things around immediately. He was pretty emotional this morning."

"There's a big surprise! If emotional intelligence were taxed, he'd get a rebate!"

"I'm meeting with him again this afternoon. I've got to come up with a way for him to get what we're doing. Do you have any plans for lunch?"

"No."

"Let's go grab a sandwich and brainstorm how to get Doug onside."

Pete and Jon kicked around various options over lunch and decided that the best thing would be for Pete to show Doug the convoluted and complicated process map developed by Li's Process Management team. Jon's Decision Making and Accountability team had been building off that work to trace the roots of the red-tape bureaucracy that was slowing everything down. The process paths on the overlapping maps looked like plates of spaghetti as they traced the "is now" or current flow of interactions and steps. The maps clearly showed how often people were forced to make arbitrary and knee-jerk decisions just to get something – anything – done in response to customer problems, service requests, errors, and everything else.

Through their involvement with the team, Li and Richard's people were now reducing the mistrust and emotionally charged elements in their interactions and learning to work together. Jason's training and guidance were helping team members use fact-based approaches to "speak with data." They were learning how to focus on the specific issue or process step, and dramatically reduce accusations, generalizations, and judgmental statements.

The teams also found some "low-hanging fruit" – process improvements they could implement immediately to quickly reduce errors and miscommunication. These rapid and visible payoffs encouraged and energized everyone to work harder at getting to the root causes of the major process bottlenecks. Many of those were within operations' control. But a few of the key contributors to process problems were embedded in company-wide policies, support systems (like information technology, human resources, procurement, or accounting), sales and marketing approaches, and senior management's planning, priority setting, and decision making.

Pete needed to get Doug onside to allow the teams to get deeper into these larger, systemic issues.

"It's a powerful picture that tells a very compelling story," Pete said when he and Jon were back in his office reviewing the maps, charts, and key data they'd printed out. "I sure hope Doug has calmed down and will be a bit more receptive."

"He can't do anything but support all this great work once he sees this," Jon said. He told Pete he was still amazed and puzzled by how the company had managed to slowly strangle itself with local fixes, "work-around strategies," and narrow departmental improvements. It was a tangled mess that had tied everything in knots.

"Mr. Drake will see you now," Rhonda announced with a smirk as she emerged from Doug's office. As she sat down at her desk, Pete noted with a bit of relief that her hands and legs were human. He thanked her and walked into Doug's office.

"So what have you come up with, Leonard?" Doug said. "It had better be good."

"How about savings of thirty to forty percent and an increase of fifty percent in customer response time in operations' work order and dispatching process, just to get started?"

"Really? You've done that already?"

"Not yet. But that's the projection of the team working on just one process. We have a few others showing as much promise. Here, let me show you."

Pete pulled on the process maps, charts, and data that he and Jon had compiled. Doug paid more attention this time as Pete walked him through the story that was emerging.

"... and the team is finding that ..."

"So just who is responsible for this *%#_^ mess?"

"No one person is responsible. It's The 85/15 Rule. Eighty-five to ninety percent of the time problems like this come from the system, process, or structure ..."

"Don't give me a bunch of academic mumbo jumbo. Who are you holding *accountable* for getting operations into this state?" Doug's face was reddening. Was that Doug's double chin or a fur bell quivering at his neckline?

"Through the kind of work you see here, we're developing much greater openness and brainstorming techniques because we're reducing fear of reprisals. We're not out to point fingers and fix blame. We're making great progress because we're focused on fixing the problems ..."

"Just as I suspected, Leonard!" Doug was bellowing now. "No one is in charge and no one is accountable! That's exactly how you got operations into this deep shit pit! And through your lack of leadership, everyone's wallowing in it."

Doug's moustache was heaving up and down as he took in short sharp breaths. Pete half expected to see flames scorch it.

"Well it is time for decision making and accountability, all right. You're finished, Leonard."

"What do you mean?"

"I mean you no longer work here. I'm letting you go. *You're fired.* As required by law, in lieu of notice, I have prepared a severance package for you. Not that you deserve it for leading us into this quagmire." He threw an envelope on the desk in front of Pete, then picked up his phone. "I am calling security to escort you to your office to clean out your desk."

Pete made a few more attempts to reason with Doug. At every word, Doug cut him off and refused to discuss his decision further. "It was clear to me in our last management meeting that you wanted a shootout. Well, you got it. I drew first and you're dead."

"Goodbye, Mr. Leonard," Rhonda said with an even bigger smirk as the security guard ushered Pete out of Doug's office.

The security guard gave Pete a large cardboard box to pack up his things. Jon was shocked when he dropped into Pete's office and heard what had just transpired. Pete tried to have brief conversations with a few others who dropped by his office as word spread, but the security guard cut them off and reminded Pete he was under strict orders to have him out of the building immediately.

Pete stuffed the rest of his personal belongings into the box and turned out the office light. He put on his moose glasses for a quick look around. He saw the huge bull moose that had been following Doug around contentedly chewing its cud in the far corner with eyes half closed. Rosie shook Pete's hand in the hallway outside his office, but choked on her words and started to cry.

When Pete started his car, the Beatles song "Blackbird" was playing. He loved that song. As he exited the parking lot in bright afternoon sunshine, he reflected on the line, "You were only waiting for this moment to be free."

To Boldly Grow

June was Pete's favorite month. It was fresh and new. It was full of the promise of warm summer days ahead. In June, sunshine-filled days started well before most people got out of bed and lasted until late into the evening. In June, everything was lush and green. Peonies, roses, phlox, irises, lilacs, lilies, clematis: a June garden is a delightful explosion of color and sweet fragrances.

How did I get so out of touch with the wonder and joy of working in our perennial garden? he wondered. He was puttering around pruning and pulling weeds in the early-morning sun. Over the past few years, Michelle had taken over more and more of the garden work as Pete grew out of touch with her, the garden, his job, and his life.

Pete couldn't figure out why he felt so alive. He had been fired the day before. He was trying to rationalize the reality of unemployment with the feeling of freedom and energy he was feeling. Years of conditioning were telling him he should feel terrible. Depressed even. But for the first time in years, he was invigorated and optimistic.

When Pete got home the night before, he and Michelle took a long walk. They weren't too far up the street when Michelle turned to him and asked what was wrong. At first Pete struggled to say the words. But the look on Michelle's face was so supportive that he just took a deep breath and said it.

"It's over."

"What's over?" Michelle said as the blood drained from her face. "Us?"

"God no," Pete said quickly, realizing those weren't the right words to start any conversation with Michelle, given their recent history. "My job. It's over."

Michelle clutched her chest in mock distress. "Oh, Pete, you almost gave me a heart attack. What happened?"

Pete told her of his "shootout" with Doug. He was surprised when she just gave him a hug and said it would all work out. "In the hero's journey," she said, "it's the adversity that gives us a chance to see what he's made of."

"I don't feel like much of a hero. More like the *fallen hero*, cut down just as I was rising to the challenge."

"Pete, the timeless wisdom found in so many modern stories and ancient myths is that we're defined more by how we handle our problems and setbacks than by our successes. The hero often learns that life's about controlling his or her own destiny or someone else will. We either live by our own belief system or we're controlled by someone else's. Whatever possessions, money, or position we have can easily be lost. But what we become is ours forever. We are rich or poor by what we are, not by what we have."

"Yeah, I guess you're right," Pete replied. "It's true that over the years I slipped into being controlled by my fear and insecurity. But I really thought operations had turned the corner. I could *feel* it. But just as it looked like we were beginning to get things under control, Doug seemed more and more determined to drag me over to the dark side. It's like he expects the worst of everyone and manages people down to his low expectations."

"He is Darth Vader – your evil nemesis," Michelle said, cupping her hands over her mouth and nose and breathing heavily. "Your power is strong, young Jedi." Laughing, she said, "Let's hope he doesn't turn out to be your father!"

Pete paused to watch a bee buzz lazily onto a rose. It walked around gathering pollen on its legs. I've just experienced the worst Doug can throw at me and it's not so bad, he thought. In fact, this could be a real blessing in disguise. This could be a chance for me to start fresh. I can apply my experience and learning to an organization that needs and values them.

"Hey, Mr. Lionhearted. Let me hear your mighty roar!"

Pete dropped his pruning shears. He spun around to see Alfred sitting on a large rock by the small pond and waterfall in the backyard. In the bright sunlight, his light moustache and the beard strip tracing his sharp chin were barely visible. The arrows were in his quiver shook as he bobbed his bare blond head. Alfred was grinning broadly. He quickly stood up to face Pete. His right foot slipped into the pond.

"So much for the grand entrance of my grand finale," Alfred said, shaking water off his tanned leather boot.

"Hey! Alfred! I haven't seen you in a while. I've *almost* missed you."

"You don't need me any more. You rediscovered your courage."

"Whether you're a figment of my imagination or real, you've been a big help. Thanks."

Alfred smiled and slightly bowed his head.

"Thanks to you I've found that facing my fears without compromising my values is one of life's most rewarding experiences. Although maybe not financially – I was just fired. Does Elric have any openings?"

"I don't think you've quite developed enough elf-esteem just yet," Alfred said with a chuckle. "Years from now you'll be more disappointed by the things you didn't do than the things you did. You certainly won't regret taking a stand for something you knew was right."

"What happened to your snazzy hat with the big feather?"

"Who are you talking to, Pete?" Michelle called across the yard as she emerged from the house. Pete quizzically shook the water from his soaked right shoe as he pondered his response.

Over the next few weeks, Pete updated his résumé and began applying for management jobs that matched his skills and experience. He treated weekday business hours as his workday. His job was to find a new job. During his lunches at home (when he wasn't out networking), in the evening, and on weekends, he invested time reading leadership and personal-growth material as well as keeping a diary of his thoughts, learnings, and key insights. During this process he found a few very helpful personal-growth and career-development books, articles, and web sites.

The following weekend – after a week of numerous phone calls, networking lunches, and two promising job interviews – Pete found a visioning exercise particularly useful. Looking out five years, he sketched his ideal job, family/home life, social circles, community involvement, financial picture, personal health, and spiritual connectedness. He shared his vision with Michelle and asked her to tell him what she saw for herself and both of them in those same areas. They got so caught up dreaming about what their lives could be like, it was almost midnight before they finally went to bed.

Harold was bathed in sunlight at the table by the window. He waved warmly to Pete and stood up. "Hey, Pete! It's great to see you again. You're looking terrific!"

"Hi, Harold. It's good to see you too."

Harold had asked Pete to have lunch with him at Rocky and Bullwinkle's.

"You've really lost weight," Harold said. "Getting out of NMTS obviously agrees with you."

"I have been paying more attention to what I eat and getting a lot more exercise."

"Well, you know that health is merely the slowest rate at which you can die."

Pete gave him a wry smile. "How have you been, Harold?"

"Oh, you know. We're at yet another crossroads at good old NMTS. One path leads to despair and destruction and the other to complete annihilation. Most of the time we don't have much fun. The rest of the time we have no fun at all."

"Still spreading good cheer and hope everywhere you go, I see," Pete said.

"These days I am the office optimist. Things have really gone downhill since you left. Due to budget constraints, the light at the end of the tunnel has now been switched off."

After they had ordered lunch, Harold asked him how his job search was going.

"Quite well, thanks. I am having a second interview with a company tomorrow, and I have a third interview next week with a company I am even more interested in. If that goes well, I think there may be an offer soon. It's funny, but getting fired was one of the best things to happen to me in years. It forced me to re-examine my strengths and weaknesses, clarify my career – and life – vision, and it has brought Michelle and me closer together."

"Well, your gain is our loss. Doug's become absolutely unbearable. The management team – and especially everyone in the POETS Society – saw how you stood up to him and got fired for it. So now he arrives at a 'consensus' by asking for any opposing views. Of course, never is heard a dissenting word. Essentially, he's saying, 'All those opposed to this plan please take a blindfold, a cigarette, and stand against the far wall while I take aim at your mindless input.'"

"But unless you address the real issues, the problems will get worse," Pete said.

"I agree. And they are."

"It takes a lot of courage to speak up," Pete said. "But the price of silence is much higher – especially in self-esteem. There must be a lot of moose in that office again."

Harold looked concerned. "You're not seeing moose stepping in front of your car again, are you?"

"I'm referring to Jason's metaphor of Moose on the Table."

"Yeah, there are plenty of Moose on the Table."

Cy Garnet called Pete the next afternoon. After a few pleasantries, he said he really needed to talk to him and asked him to lunch the next day. Pete had an interview that day, so they agreed to meet on Thursday. Why in the world would Doug's boss be calling me? Pete wondered as he hung up the phone.

Taming of the Zoo

"Hi Cy! It's great to see you again!" Pete stood to shake Cy's hand as he found his way to the table.

"Sorry I'm late, Pete. Things are getting pretty crazy around the office these days."

"So I hear."

"You're looking terrific. Have you been working out?"

"Thanks. I'm not pumping iron, but I've made a few lifestyle changes I should have made years ago."

Cy ordered a Coke and Pete ordered cranberry juice mixed with club soda.

"That sounds pretty healthy," Cy said.

"Yeah. I sure am finding that we are what we eat and drink."

"Pete, I'll get right to the point. The reason I asked to meet with you is because I want to offer you the position of senior vice president."

"Really? Are you kidding? That's Doug's position."

"Not anymore. I let him go a few days ago. I should have done it much, much sooner. But he really played me like a fiddle. Now that I see the full picture, I feel like a complete fool. Doug was clearly a master at kissing up and kicking down. He told me and the board exactly what we wanted to hear. He was very good with our key clients. They loved him. He also impressed our bankers with his take-charge, decisive demeanor. They considered him a real leader."

The waiter arrived with their drinks and asked for their lunch order. Pete ordered a large spinach salad topped with nuts, and strips of grilled teriyaki salmon with low-fat dressing on the side. "I'll have the same," Cy said. "It's clearly working for this guy."

Cy jumped right back into his story. "I was getting more and more uncomfortable with Doug's leadership after Heather began updating me on the big turnaround you were orchestrating in operations. The day he fired you, I was at sea on the first day of a cruise vacation. I promised myself and Irene – given all the stress of the past year – that this really was a vacation and I wouldn't check e-mail. It was almost a week after you were fired that I read Heather's e-mail. She said we couldn't afford to lose you at this critical juncture."

Cy took a long sip of Coke and glanced briefly out the window. "Once I got back to the office I went to work on getting to the bottom of this whole mess. I had been so consumed by our financial crisis that I'd grown out of touch with what was happening throughout the company. Since you seemed to be on your way back to a strong leadership position, turning things around in operations, I was paying even less attention to what was going on in your area."

Turning back to Pete, he said, "You certainly have a bunch of very loyal supporters. Harold, Rosie, and Duncan took some real risks in approaching me. Each one did so independently. They initiated those courageous conversations that Jason Reynard writes and talks about so well. All three of them strongly objected to your firing and told me how Doug was actually running things and treating people. Somehow Doug caught wind of Duncan's support for you. Heather alerted me that Doug was having HR prepare Duncan's severance package. I immediately contacted Doug and put a stop to it."

Pete could just imagine Doug's quivering double-chin clapper during that interaction.

Cy continued, "I also heard about Jon's process-management research and went to see him to find out about what he and his team had been learning. He gave me the presentation that you and he prepared for Doug. Very impressive and enlightening! We clearly need to act on those findings immediately.

"Then I met with Doug to discuss your firing. He presented a flimsy case for why he let you go. So the picture was complete. I clearly saw that we had a very weak senior VP who got rid of you because you were standing up to him and using approaches that contradicted his bullying style. His fear and insecurity drove him to shut down any dissent or real discussions."

Their salads arrived.

"I then had to get to work covering our bases with key customers. So over the last few weeks – in preparation for letting Doug go – I worked hard to strengthen relationships with a few key clients who were particularly attached to Doug. It was tricky because Doug had built almost exclusive relationships with them and was trying to keep me away. We couldn't afford for them to get skittish when I dismissed him. I also had to alert our bankers to what I was planning to do, and why, so they wouldn't suddenly pull the plug. That incredible Clockroaches memo sure helped. If you accept the job, they want to meet with you as soon as possible."

"I am flattered by your offer, Cy. But for your sake and mine, I've got to ensure this is the right move at this point in my life. Could I have a few days to think this over and talk to Michelle?"

"Of course."

"So what are you going to do about the job offer?" Michelle asked him on their evening walk.

"It's an embarrassment of riches. A couple of the other jobs I'm up for are very appealing. But this senior VP role is a great opportunity to build on the experience and work I started in operations. But if I do go back, it will be on my terms."

Later that evening Pete was reviewing his career-planning notes and journal reflections. Michelle put her hand on his shoulder and asked, "Is my beloved hero looking back on his road of trials to decide which direction to take ahead on his road back?"

"Yeah, something like that," Pete said. "Most of all, I want to ensure that if I take this position, I'm doing it as an extension of my values and strengths, and not just for the power, prestige, and money. I want to master my job from a position of alignment, so that the job doesn't – once again – master me."

"You know I couldn't resist doing a bit of research on Cy Garnet's name," Michelle said. "'Cyril' is the Greek form of a Persian name that may mean 'far-sighted.' Given that he hired Doug and let that situation get so badly out of control, I'm not sure that fits. However, 'Garnet' comes from an Old English surname meaning 'hinge,' as originally denoting a person who sold hinges."

When Pete was escorted out of NMTS, he had no expectation of ever darkening its doors again. But now here he was sitting with Cy chit-chatting about their families and summer vacations – just like the old days. Pete thought about how Cy's modest office created a much more positive and action-oriented environment than Doug's fake palatial suite.

About ten minutes in, Cy asked Pete if he was going to accept the job offer.

"As I said on the phone, I'm certainly interested in pursuing it further," Pete said. "But if I am going to take it on, I want to do it very differently than Doug did. Since I haven't reported directly to you for years – and our personal and company circumstances are dramatically different – I'd like to see if you would support the approach I'd want to take."

Cy was all ears. "We certainly do need to do things differently around here," he said. "If we keep doing what we've been doing, we'll keep getting the lousy results we've been getting. So what are your conditions for getting back on board and taking the helm?"

"They aren't conditions so much as ensuring that you'd support what I'd want to do and how I would do it." Pete pulled a notepad from his small blue satchel. "I've got a few notes."

"Okay. Shoot."

"All right. As you know, we really need more office space. I also want to spend much more time actively leading people and much less time managing things – especially chained to my desk dealing with e-mails. Rather than moving into Doug's regal suite, I want to turn it into a mapping and planning room for our improvement teams. I'll be 'hoteling.' That means I won't have an office. Using mobile technology, I'll set up where ever I find a spot or in one of our other meeting rooms when I need privacy."

"That's a bit radical, but I can see where you're going with this approach. If I am not using my office, you can come in here too."

"Okay, thanks. I also need you to buy into dealing with all the moose – no matter how sacred they may be. We have some major corporate issues that are getting in the way of our departments and teams. This will inevitably lead right up to you, the board, our clients, and maybe even our bankers. I need you to be prepared to put everything on the table."

"I don't know, Pete. I can't just give you a blank check on that one," Cy responded with a worried look.

"Cy, we need to open up everything to discussion and debate. Are you prepared to have open conversations and act on what clearly needs to be done?"

"Pete, there are some non-negotiables in the way this company is run."

"And that's where the moose love to hide. We may not be able to control or change some of those things, but we have to put them on the table to explore our options. When we see these issues for what they are, they lose power."

"I'm concerned about how far this will go, and how productive it's going to be when what we really need is less talk and more action."

"I strongly agree that we need action. But that action has to be based on a proper analysis that gets at the root causes or systemic origins of many of our biggest problems. We've got to stop running madly around slapping band-aids on a bunch of symptoms without fixing the underlying conditions. We've got lots of action now, but it's helter-skelter."

"I guess that's true."

"So we need to harness the collective brainpower and experience of everyone to really understand what's going on. Then we need everyone's strong buy-in and commitment to implementing the big changes we need to make. As Jason Reynard says, 'If they help plan the battle, they are less likely to battle the plan.'"

"I can see that."

"We've had way too much going-along-to-get-along and inauthentic conversations around here. This behavior has attracted a major herd of moose that are getting in the way and slowing us down. We need loud debates, heated conflict, and healthy arguments."

"That's the part I am having real trouble with. We have enough problems now. I don't see how more conflict is a good thing."

"Let me give you an example. Two Saturdays ago, Ryan was home from university. It's a rare treat to have him home, so we tried to figure out what to do for some nice family time together. It's been a while since we did anything together, so the ideas weren't exactly plentiful. After a bit of overly polite discussion, the four of us agreed to pile in our car and drive ninety minutes to the zoo. It took three hours to get back, due to a huge traffic jam. I think the whole trip was mostly for old time's sake. At the zoo, we spent four hours trudging around from pavilion to pavilion – in the rain – looking at exhibits that hadn't changed in years.

"It was a quiet ride there and a sullen ride back. As we sat there stuck in traffic seven dismal hours later, we finally vented our true feelings. Cy, *not one us* had wanted to go to the zoo in the first place. Everybody was being too polite and going along with what they thought the others wanted to do. If we'd had an open conversation about how everyone really felt, we would have had a much better time together."

"Been there, done that," Cy said with a chuckle.

"We've been on way too many trips to the zoo around here. We need to learn how to argue without being argumentative.

We have to learn how to attack all sides of the issue without attacking each other. That's a huge culture change for us."

"Yes, it is. We do avoid voicing disagreement and differences of opinion – to each other's faces anyway."

"That's for sure. We need frank and very open communication on our financial crisis. We have to stop trying to 'motivate' people with lofty visions and varnished truths about our dire predicament. If we're ever going to turn things around, we must build an open and fear-free environment where we can all work together."

"I am uncomfortable about what you're proposing," Cy replied. "But maybe that's the way it should be. We've become just a little too comfortable and set in our ways. And obviously avoiding the issues hasn't worked. We do go to the zoo a little too often. "

"So we've got to engage everyone in turning this company around. We need to get an LFA process going immediately."

"I know Jason is a big advocate of that approach. Remind me again what it is."

"I was just refreshing myself on it last night from one of his books. It's Listen-Feedback-Action. Basically it starts with a survey and/or focus groups to gather systematic input on the key issues that need to be addressed. Once that data is compiled and summarized, it's fed back to everyone in a series of open forums or 'town hall' meetings. Teams then identify improvement actions they're going to take and send action ideas up to the corporate level for broader implementation."

"Do we have the time to do something as extensive as that?"

"We already have some survey data that we could supplement with a few focus groups, e-mail surveys, and one-on-one interviews by a neutral, outside consultant. It would take some upfront time – which I am sure we could cut down. But the real time savings come in the time to implement because everyone is now on board, understands what needs to be done, and can go straight back and do it. I'd want to couple the input we gather with the process and other data-driven analysis that the operations Strategic Imperative teams have developed."

"I can see that. Well, Pete, you've clearly thought this through. You're making me squirm with some of what you want to do, but I am even more convinced now that we need your leadership. Are you on-board?"

"If you support what I am planning to do, then yes, I'd do it at the drop of a hat."

"Terrific!" Cy rose from his chair and extended his hand. Pete grasped it and they firmly shook hands.

"Let's do it!" Cy said.

In the Winner's Cycle

WELCOME BACK, MIGHTY MOOSE HUNTER!

The large banner was hung on the back wall of the office. A hand-drawn longbow and quiver of arrows adorned the left corner. The right corner featured a bright orange hunting vest. As Pete entered the office a week after his meeting with Cy, he took in the banner and about fifteen managers and staff people standing around the sign. They broke into applause as he approached them.

"Let's hear it for Pete the Lionhearted," Harold bellowed. "Hip, hip, hooray! Hip, hip, hooray! Hip, hip, hooray!"

Everyone cheered in unison and applauded again as they finished.

"Whoa! I appreciate the warm reception. But I think you're going *way* over the top here," Pete said.

"Speech, speech!" Rosie said.

"Now you're really putting me on the spot," Pete replied. "I still have a lot of improvement work to do. And improving my public speaking is right at the top of my self-development list. I'm flattered by this reception. But I've heard it said that flattery is like aftershave. It smells good, feels brisk and tingly – but is fatal if swallowed."

An appreciative chuckle rippled through the group.

"I am delighted to be back and working with such a great group of people. Many of you played a part in naming and hunting our moose. And we've got lots more hunting to do if we're going to turn this company around."

The welcoming party continued for another fifteen minutes before everyone slowly drifted back to their desks.

"Hi, Pete! How's your first day back in the swamp?" Rosie popped her frizzy head into the conference room. It was mid-afternoon and Pete had played host to many familiar faces welcoming him back throughout the day.

"It feels like this is exactly where I should be. There's certainly no shortage of things to do."

"That's for sure. And you're just the leader to take us forward. The POETS Society is meeting at Rocky and Bullwinkle's for a drink. Our main task is to rename the society. Can you join us?"

"For a short bit. Michelle and I have a dinner date tonight. We have some celebrating to do."

"See you there."

"Here's our conquering hero. Hail Caesar!" Chuck raised his flying squirrel tankard to salute Pete. Others joined in greeting him. It looked like the entire senior management team that Pete was now leading, along with his old operations management team, were there. Tables had been pushed together to form one large group.

Rosie clanked a spoon against a glass as she rose from her chair. "Your attention, please. I know Pete only has a few minutes with us before he leaves for a hot date." She grinned at Pete. "The main reason we're here is to rename the POETS Society. Until this momentous day, it was the Piss-On-Everything-Till-Sunrise Society. The floor is now open for new name suggestions."

"How about Pete's-Our-Executive-and-Total-Savior."

"I'd veto that one," Pete said. "Your expectations for me are getting way too high. Remember, as far as we've traveled the past few months, we're truly just beginning. The really hard part of our journey is just ahead. And we're going to have to clear out our moose together."

"What about Pave-Over-Everything-in-The-Swamp?"

"Now there's a really environmentally sensitive thought!"

"Put-Our-Energy-Toward-Shooting moose instead of each other," Harold said, raising his glass to Duncan down the table. Duncan smiled and raised his mug in return.

"Praise-On-Everything-Till-Sunrise."

"Pete's-Only..."

The next few months involved some of the hardest work that Pete had ever done. The hours were long and the discussions were difficult. Pete took a few intensive days of training filled with lots of practice and feedback to improve his speaking and presentation skills. It was a grueling and somewhat ego-bruising exercise. In the end the payoff was huge. Pete would look back years later and say it was one of the most significant personal-growth investments he'd ever made.

The training left Pete with a much greater degree of confidence on his feet, whether in front of two or two hundred people. He also learned how to pull together a series of his personal stories and perspectives that powerfully connected with his audience's hearts.

"We need their heads and best thinking," he explained to Michelle on one of their evening walks. "But we can't just think our way out of this mess to bring about the culture and organizational changes we so desperately need. We must have everybody's passion and emotional energy to fuel the courageous conversations going on up, down, across, out, and all around our company."

Working with Jason and Heather's guidance and co-facilitation, Pete embarked on an extensive Listen-Feedback-Action process to reach everyone within the client services division. They began by pulling out key themes from the organizational survey that Heather and the HR group had put together earlier in the year.

Pete then organized front-line staff groups in small town-hall meetings within head office and out in all the regional offices. He began with a few personal stories drawn from his early days at NMTS and the difficult challenges they overcame. He then openly related his drift toward going-along-to-get-along and apathy. He talked about his weak moose-hunting attempts and how he finally built up the courage to get serious about tackling the biggest issues – and especially his own leadership shortcomings.

He put a positive spin on getting fired and worked hard not to show Doug in a negative light. Since most people loathed Doug and had heard grapevine versions of Pete's courageous behaviors with Doug, Pete's generous comments toward Doug and his experiences strengthened their respect for him.

After Pete reviewed the early survey results and other data that the strategic imperative teams had collected, the meetings then moved from the feedback to action phase. Jason or Heather alternated sessions with Pete. He actively led every one of the nineteen meetings over a six-week period. Jason and Heather worked with Pete to collect small- and large-group brainstorming ideas. These were clustered into common themes and further discussed within the groups. Everything was recorded and eventually summarized and synthesized with all the other notes.

"Wow! The input is pretty clear and consistent! It also shows that our earlier work in operations mirrors these issues pretty well," Pete said as he reviewed the notes Heather and Jason had pulled together a few days after the last town-hall meeting. They were in a small conference room that Pete had booked for their meeting. A small stuffed moose was sitting on the table.

The notes showed that the biggest moose issues to be addressed were client service levels, communications, priority overload, departmental silos, system and process misalignment (which included decision making), and accountability and follow-through.

"I've got some strong opinions on how we deal with these," Pete said to Heather and Jason. "But first I'd like to hear yours."

"We have been talking about an implementation strategy and put together this outline," Jason said, dropping a short document in front of Pete.

The paper sketched in broad terms how they could realign the Strategic Imperative teams to cut across the whole organization.

"Pete would chair the overall divisional steering team consisting of the leaders from each Strategic Imperative team and Pete's management team," Jason said. "I recommend we start with getting your new management team together for an off-site planning session similar to what you did with the operations management team at Elkhorn Lodge. "I'd do an overview of that leadership and organization development material we covered. We would then review this town-hall meeting report and fill in the details of a double-track plan."

Jason went on to explain that one track would be quick actions that could be taken to get immediate payoffs and quick wins. This would build momentum and boost energy for the long-term changes covered in the other track. "If we're really targeted and do it right, we'll also free up many people's time and significant company dollars from all the wasted efforts now going into rework, resolving client issues, miscommunication problems, errors – or what in our business we call 'cost of poor quality.'"

They talked through more options and ways to approach the double-track implementation.

"Okay," Pete said as he sat back in his chair. "Let's get that management-planning session together. Heather, can you please get right on that? I'll get dates to you both by the end of the day, once I've talked to each of the managers."

Two and a half weeks later the management team – after furious calendar juggling – had their off-site planning session at a local hotel. It was a highly productive few days of visioning, consensus building, team building, and planning. Each of the Strategic Imperative teams was refocused and members were changed and shuffled to cut across the entire company. Each team was asked to produce a short-term "Quick Wins" plan within three weeks for the divisional steering team.

Right on time, the plans were reviewed and agreed to with few changes. The divisional steering team was very impressed with how thoughtful and potentially effective the plans appeared to be.

Pete was finishing up one of his last town-hall updates, meeting in the company cafeteria. Through a smaller number of much larger meetings, he had managed to reach everyone in their sprawling division with a brief overview of all that was now going on following the LFA sessions they had participated in a month or so before. Each of the Strategic Imperative team leaders also gave updates on the focus and progress of their teams. Pete then wrapped up with the management team's long-term vision for clients services and specific next steps.

He outlined how over the next few months everyone would participate in a one-day program entitled "The NMTS Way."

"The purpose of the program is to expand on our the vision and values, and the ways all of us in management heard you tell us we should be treating each other and our customers," he explained. "The NMTS Way will become the foundation on which we'll build our long-term culture. All of our hiring, promotions, performance management, training, customer service, and key personal, team, and organizational leadership practices will build from this program."

There was a ripple of applause at this.

"Thanks for coming out today and thanks for all your patience and input. We're getting rid of lots of moose. Let's keep that up and let's not go to the zoo like my family did on that rainy day!"

Pete scanned the group. "So stay tuned," he said. "You ain't seen nothin' yet!"

The feeling in the room was electric as attendees rose to their feet and delivered a thunderous ovation.

Hat Tricks

Pete and Cy were just finishing their meeting with Nic and Monica, the company bankers, to review the company's latest financial statements.

"Pete, hats off to you," Nic said. "We're very impressed with what you've done. Thanks to your leadership, NMTS is back on track."

"Thanks, Nic. I appreciate that. But it wouldn't have happened if it wasn't for Cy's mentoring years ago and his solid support and counsel to me over the past few months."

Pete and Cy had scheduled regular weekly meetings or conference calls to discuss issues and progress. This helped keep Cy in the loop and gave him confidence that Pete's approach was actually working. Because of this, while Pete continued to build from within, Cy took on extensive client relationship building and worked to keep the board, corporate executives, suppliers, bankers, the press, and other key outside players onside.

"I did get badly off-track with Doug," Cy said. "Pete's transformed and inspired leadership was exactly what we needed. There were times I squirmed through tough conversations as difficult issues were being addressed. But the proof is certainly in the results we see here today. And I know this is just the beginning. Our conservative projections for the next four quarters show us sharply accelerating our profit. We're going to be generating so much cash, we'll start lending your bank money – if your leadership plan is up to snuff!"

Everyone laughed.

After the bankers left, Pete and Cy continued with their weekly meeting.

"I understand you've rehired Damali," Cy said.

"Yes, and I'm really excited to have her back on-board. She's such a strong accounting executive. She stayed in touch with people here and heard good things about what was going on. When I approached her about returning, she was quite receptive."

"It's another great example of that research showing how people join a company and quit their boss," Cy said. "We lost a lot of good people during Doug's reign of terror – my reign of error."

"We're rebuilding and either getting some of the good ones back or bringing on even stronger replacements," Pete said. "The exodus of our best techs has stopped. We're not yet a 'magnet organization' – attracting and retaining the best people – as described in our vision, but we're well on our way."

"I can't get over the change in Rhonda. She was so loyal to Doug. You've really turned her around."

"She did offer to resign the first week I was here. I must admit I was tempted to accept after the way she gloated when Doug fired me. But I also knew she had a lot of experience and organizational knowledge that we could really use. So I sat down with her and had a clear – and tough – conversation about my expectations for her behavior. She was badly tainted by Doug's blustery style and abuse of power. I had to have two follow-up conversations with her about The NMTS Way when she was drifting back into old habits in dealing with some people. She responded well and has proven to be invaluable to the teams working on our management processes."

"Well, it's been fabulous to see your rebirth as such a strong leader. The next few years are going to be really interesting around here. You've really grown to fill the hat of leadership."

"Or my head is swelling," Pete chuckled. "I certainly agree with you. We've only just begun."

"Your personal and organizational turnaround is quite a story. I know many people are inspired by your courageous leadership."

"Thanks, Cy. It's been quite a ride over the past six months. The process wasn't very pretty and even quite bizarre as I headed down a path of elf ... uh ... I mean self-destruction. But eventually some much needed learning – and re-learning – did get through to me." Pete glanced at his watch. "Whoa, look at the time. I've got to get going."

As Pete left the office building, he caught his reflection in the first-floor office windows. He stopped dead and stared. Alfred's hat was on his head! The black-and-white feather was waving merrily in the light breeze. Pete put his hand on his head. It was bare. He gazed intently at his hat-topped reflection. Then, with a knowing smile and a wink, he continued on his way, walking straight and tall with confidence and purpose.

Now get online and find the tools — and do some moose hunting of your own!

www.clemmer.net   www.moose-on-the-table.ca

You've just read the book, now follow Pete Leonard's example and take action. Go from inspiration to application.

We've pulled together all sorts of free resources on our web site to help you track and address the moose in your team or organization.

Videos
Choose from dozens of free clips of Jim addressing various topics, using the timeless principles of leadership effectiveness.

Articles
Browse through hundreds of articles that are sure to energize and inspire. Send them to your friends and colleagues or use them in your newsletter or magazine, completely free of charge.

Blog
Keep up with Jim's latest thoughts and activities on leadership and management at his frequently updated blog.

eNewsletters
Sign up for Jim's complimentary *Leader Letter* and receive a monthly digest of articles posted on his blog. Or get more frequent inspiration three times a week when you sign up for Jim's *Improvement Points*.

Keynotes, workshops, and team retreats
You'll find a comprehensive set of personal, team, and organizational-development topics (including moose hunting) that Jim will customize to help you develop a culture of leadership in your organization. Contact us for a free assessment and learn how you can make a real difference today.

Books, audios, and other resources
Our online store has all of Jim's resources together in one place. Buy books and download material for yourself, or take advantage of deep discounts when you purchase quantities of 10 or more for your team.

Keep learning, laughing, loving, and leading – living life just for the L of it!

GROWING THE DISTANCE
Timeless Principles for
Personal, Career, and Family Success

With over 100,000 copies in print, *Growing the Distance* clearly hit a nerve.

Change is all around us – our families, workplaces, and society are in a state of constant flux. *Growing the Distance* puts forth two choices. We can be victims of change or meet challenges head-on by changing ourselves.

This highly readable book takes readers on a journey to develop the leadership qualities that often lie dormant in each and every one of us.

Through humorous quips, anecdotes, and insightful commentary, Jim builds on his decades of experience in leadership and personal development to create a remarkably easy-to-read guide to living and growing that moves readers from inspiration to application.

Visit our web site (www.clemmer.net) and you'll find much of *Growing the Distance* excerpted as short articles freely available for you to read and forward to friends and colleagues.

THE LEADER'S DIGEST
Timeless Principles for
Team and Organization Success

Personal growth is a twisting path winding its way through every aspect of life. Once we make the choice to follow this path, everything changes.

As a follow-up and companion to *Growing the Distance*, *The Leader's Digest* expands the canvas to help readers grow from leading self to leading others – using inner wisdom to guide outward actions.

Whether used for a small workforce or large multinational, *The Leader's Digest* employs the same wit and style of its predecessor to help readers hone the skills necessary to make a significant difference at home or in the workplace.

To learn more about Jim's other books, read free articles, or sign up for his monthly newsletter, visit www.clemmer.net.

CPSIA information can be obtained at www.ICGtesting.com
228269LV00008B/72/P

9 780978 222178